Mrs. P.A Henry

Memoir of the Rev. Thomas Henry

Mrs. P.A Henry
Memoir of the Rev. Thomas Henry
ISBN/EAN: 9783337132408
Printed in Europe, USA, Canada, Australia, Japan
Cover: Foto ©ninafisch / pixelio.de

More available books at **www.hansebooks.com**

MEMOIR

OF

REV. THOMAS HENRY

CHRISTIAN MINISTER, YORK PIONEER,

AND SOLDIER OF 1812.

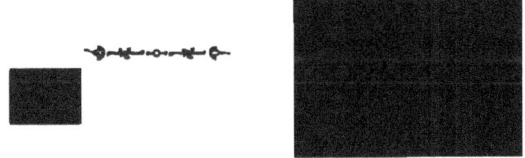

WRITTEN AND PUBLISHED BY HIS DAUGHTER-IN-LAW,

Mrs. P. A. HENRY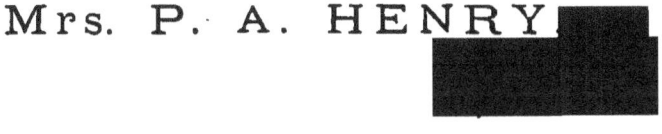

Toronto:
HILL & WEIR, STEAM PRINTERS, 15, 17 AND 19 TEMPERANCE STREET.
1880.

PREFACE.

In all this great, crowded, busy world, no man lives to himself alone, but to the world. Every life is an influence cast upon society by which it is made better or worse. Neither does that influence cease when the pulse of natural life ceases to beat; every man leaves an impression on some page of the world's history. In proportion as the man is great and active, so will the impression be lasting and extensive. Good or bad, this influence is inevitable, and goes on in widening circles, like the ripple from a pebble dropped in water, until its swell reaches the shores of eternity.

The subject of this sketch was a good man, and great in the true sense of the word. "Though dead he yet speaketh." His memory is warm in the hearts of hundreds in this Province, and long will the influence of his life of integrity and devotion to the right be felt. It is a power for good; and to widen and increase that power have we prepared and now offer to the public, this little work. To those who knew and loved him, and all who love or appreciate real moral uprightness, it is dedicated. That the blessing of the God whom he served may attend it, is the prayer of

THE AUTHOR.

CHAPTER I.

INTRODUCTION—EARLY LIFE.

YES, Father Henry is gone! The great man who stood like a tower of strength in our midst, is not here. The hand that was ever ready to help, is stretched out to us no more. The lips we loved to kiss are cold; and the voice whose sound was music and wisdom to us, we hear not. The dear and revered head lies on its pillow of earth.

Our hearts, under the first sense of their great want and bereavement, cry out against it. Oh Death! what hast thou done? Father in Heaven, was it Thou? Didst Thou send the Dark Boatman to dip his oar in the waves of time, and bring him we loved into the "white calm" of Thy eternal presence?

"Forever with the Lord;
Amen so let it be!"

It is well with thee, O father! and it will be well with all, who like thee, tread conscientiously in the path of duty. It is well that the bright spring time, and the gorgeous summer months are succeeded by the golden, fruit-crowned autumn, and the brooding snows of winter.

And it *is well*, though our hearts cry out in pain against it, that thou hast been gathered, like a ripe cluster in the glorious autumnal days; or like the full, grain-laden sheaf into the garner of our God!

It is well with Father Henry; and we will bear it in mind as we turn again the pages of the past, and gather up some fragments of the history of his eventful life. Whether that life-path led up the rugged steeps of time, or through its pleasant valleys, or bordered on the stormy deep, it was well with him, for he did his work well, and bore the cross ever onward through sun and storm.

To those who knew and loved Father Henry, we dedicate this little work. It is less a regular biography than a few loving remembrances of him.

There are old men and women, with dim eyes and trembling limbs, who will love to read about Bro. Henry, whom they have known and loved so long, and who has sympathized with them in hours of sorrow, and rejoiced in their days of rejoicing. We put our little work in large print and short chapters, that they may read and not grow weary.

There are men and women, in the strength and fulness of life, who will want to read Father Henry's memoirs, for they have known him as long as they can remember; and there are little children who will want to read about him, because he was always pleasant and spoke to them.

We will gratify these wishes by telling something of the early life of Father Henry; or, as we must call him in those early years, THOMAS HENRY.

We know little of his early youth, for he was not given to telling old stories with self for the hero. He was born in the Township of Drumless, County of Cavan, Ireland, on the 2nd of February, 1798. The second name was formerly spelled Henery, but after their removal to America the second e was dropped, and the name spelled Henry by all the younger branches of the family. Simeon Henry, the great grandfather of the subject of this sketch, lived to the great age of 103 years.

Thomas Henry, his grandfather, professed the Quaker religion. He lived to have only two children, one daughter named Mary, and one son, John, who was the father of Thomas Henry. His father was brought up under the influence of the Established Church of England; but his mother, Nancy Biggers, was a Presbyterian.

The family were loyal, and his great grandfather was buried with military honors, for service rendered the Government, in some of the rebellious outbreaks of his unhappy country. His father afterward joined the Orangemen, which at that time was a necessary precaution for the protection of himself and family.

Like thousands of his countrymen, he wearied of oppression and priestcraft, and began to look longingly across the Atlantic, towards America, where he hoped to find that boon for which humanity ever asks,—Political and Religious liberty.

Accordingly in 1811 he set sail for America with his family, consisting of a wife, four sons and three daughters. A voyage across the Atlantic was a different thing then from what it is now. After tossing about on the restless waves for seven weeks and three days, they landed in New York. It was in June, when Nature wears her most attractive garb, they reached their destination. No wonder that after their long, fatiguing sea voyage, it looked like a beautiful, as well as a New World to them.

They had some relatives in New York City, but being able to find but one, a Mr. McGee, cousin to Mrs. Henry, they remained only a few weeks in the city, whence they proceeded to Albany. Here the family suffered severely from the ague, and did not continue their journey until September. Their destination was Toronto, Ontario, then Little York, capital of Upper Canada. But what now would only be a few hours ride in a rail-car, was then a long fatiguing journey. They proceeded up the Mohawk River in a flat-bottomed boat, as far as that was practicable, and then by stage or private conveyance to Lewiston, thence by boat to Toronto. These months of travelling and sickness had nearly exhausted the parental purse. They were introduced to Gen. Brock, who afterwards fell at Queenston Heights, and others high in office, who not only used their influence in their behalf, but held out alluring promises which were never fulfilled. Those of the family who were able to earn their bread, had to go to work. Thomas, being the eldest, was hired as an attendant to Judge Powell. Here he found a good home, and as the house was frequented by those high in office, he had opportunities of learning many things that were of great benefit to him in after life. He was the Judge's attendant in various official trips, stopping with him at the homes of those highest in position in the Province. This was in 1812, the first year of the war between United States and Great Britain. These journeys were made on horseback and principally through the woods, some distance back from Lake Ontario, where the roads were mere trails marked by blazed trees. The more open and better worked road along the Lake Shore was rendered unsafe for travel, by presence of parties of Yankee soldiers at various points on the route. On one of these trips to Kingston, he formed the acquaintance of a Mr. Strachan, teacher of a High School in that place.

Judge Powell arranged with him to come to Toronto and teach there, which he did, and afterwards became widely known as Archbishop Strachan, of Toronto. The next year, when Judge Powell was succeeded by Judge Campbell, young Mr. Henry, in consideration of his knowledge of the route, was employed to attend him on an official trip to Montreal. On his way thither, while stopping at a small wayside inn, his hat was stolen, and to his great mortification he was obliged to go on to Montreal bareheaded, or at least without a hat, as such an article could not be procured for love or money between where he was and the city. He remained a month in

EARLY LIFE. 13

Montreal, formed many pleasant acquaintances, and learned something of the French language.

The next year, which was the last of the war, he hired as a substitute in the army, and did military duty until peace was restored. He was employed with others to guard a batch of American prisoners from Toronto to Kingston, and another to Fort George at Niagara. It is not probable that his experience in the army was beneficial to the moral or religious character of the young man, but he learned much of human nature, and began to develop that integrity, energy, perseverance and economy, which characterized his after life. While in the Garrison in Toronto he received, as other soldiers did, besides the regular rations, an extra bottle of spirits on Saturday night for Sunday use. While others made merry over their bottle on Sunday, he sent his to a small grocery to be sold, and carefully laid by the proceeds. We may reasonably conclude this was not the only thing in which he economized during the war, as at its close, though only seventeen, he had laid by $400.

In 1816 the elder Mr. Henry removed to Whitby, and purchased the farm at Port Oshawa, which afterwards became the home of Eld. Thomas Henry, where so many of his Christian friends have enjoyed his hospitality, where he died, and where his widow still lives.

Thomas accompanied his family to Whitby, and with his savings purchased 110 acres of land lying north of his father's farm, which is now the home of one of his sons, J. G. Henry.

At the time of the settlement of the family in Whitby it was a wilderness, inhabited chiefly by the untutored Indian, the prowling wolf and timid deer; and often the family, in their little home on the picturesque shores of Lake Ontario, were awakened at the dead of night by the Indian's wild whoop, or the howl of the hungry wolf. But the wood was pleasant when the sun gilded the tree-tops, or struggled through the boughs down into the dim mossy recesses of its silent colonades. Company was scarce, but work was plenty, and in the active employment of fitting the new farm for a home, the summer months glided rapidly away.

Autumn came and wreathed its many colored drapery around the mighty forests' head, but the bright tints faded, the red leaves fell, and when the heavy frosts came down on the bare brown earth, a great affliction fell on the little household in their lonely, forest home. The wife and mother died.

Almost without precursor or warning she went, and left anguish and desolation behind her. Far from sympathizing friends, far from religious comforters, with none but her own little family around her, she bowed her head, and closed her eyes in death. But Jesus was with her, and none can be utterly desolate who hear the voice of Him who walks on the billows of death, whispering in the dull ear, "It is I; be not afraid!"

There was no minister of religion in the Township then, but as there was one in Clark, about twenty miles distant, he was procured, and she was buried with Christian rites, on a little hill beside the lake, where now in a good old age her son has lain down beside her.

To Thomas, who was not yet eighteen, the loss was extremely severe. His mother had always been an object of reverence and affection with him, and it was no wonder that now the whole world looked dark and lonely. In society, with the amusements and incentives to action which it presents, the young soon forget their sorrows; but living retired as they were, where everything reminded him of the dear departed one, there was nothing to beguile his thoughts from his loss.

To make matters worse, his father, at the end of six months, formed another and an unhappy union. This caused the young man to arouse from his despondency, and look into the future. His home seemed no longer a home to him, and he could not content himself to remain there. He would have gone to school, for his opportunities had been limited, and he felt the need of an education; but schools were few and mostly under the control of the Family Compact, which so nearly ruled the Province then, and for years after; and it was not easy to get into a school. Business openings were scarce, and his proud spirit revolted at the idea of hiring out as a "hewer of wood and drawer of water."

He finally resolved to settle on his own land. Accordingly on the 30th of July, 1817, he was married to Elizabeth Davis, who was two years younger than himself. Notwithstanding the extreme youth of both parties, the union proved a happy one. The young lady was gentle, affectionate, and religiously inclined; while he, with his experience and natural energy, proved himself more capable of supporting and directing a family, than many men of mature years.

With a stout heart and a strong arm, he went into the woods and cut logs, and built a cabin to shelter himself and wife until a clearing could be made, and a better house built. Chopping and clearing land are no holiday work, and day after day the blows from his ringing axe sounded among the echoing tree-tops. His young wife, when unemployed by household cares, would find her way out into the wood where he was engaged, not only that she might enjoy his society, but help in the easy work of gathering the limbs of the fallen trees. Full of energy and hope, they toiled cheerfully and unitedly to prepare them a home and provide the comforts of life. They did not remain long in the log house. With a whipsaw and the assistance of another hand, he sawed lumber for a frame house, which was the third frame house erected in the township.

Conversion.

CHAPTER II.

CONVERSION AND EARLY RELIGIOUS EXPERIENCE.

ON the 6th of April, 1819, Thomas Henry and his youthful wife, looked for the first time on the face of their first born. He says, "We called her Nancy after my mother." But though warm hearts welcomed its coming, the little stranger did not linger long with them; death set his icy seal, and closed the little eyes and stiffened the tiny limbs. A group of friends and neighbors gathered, and bore the small coffin to the lonely graveyard on the hill, and interred it among the few bodies which had already been committed to that quiet dwelling place. For few as were the living inhabitants of the township, this city of the dead was beginning to be built, and to gather in its dwellers.

Mr. Henry appears to have been, when very young, the subject of religious impressions. Like most great or good men, he had a good mother, and to her he ascribes this early tendency of his mind. The means of education were scarce, and Bibles hard to be obtained ; and almost the only book to which he had access was the Book of Common Prayer, and in that he has since testified that he found much good ; but for both his mental and moral culture, he was chiefly indebted to the faithfulness and care of that noble mother. He says, "She used to impress on our minds, that there was a hell to shun, a heaven to gain, and our souls to save. And I remember when not ten years old, being concerned about my salvation." The religious impressions of childhood had never entirely forsaken him, and when he married and commenced an independent life, he resolved to dedicate it to God, and serve Him according to the best of his abilities ; but in the active labors of his busy life, time slipped away, and little religious progress had been made. But when the tendrils of parental love, which had just reached out to entwine themselves around this new-born treasure, were thus rudely snapped, it recalled his mind from its absorbing pursuit after material good, to realize that there was another and a higher good to be sought.

The Methodists had, at that time, established a church in York County, and one Elder Jackson held meetings in the vicinity of Mr. Henry's residence. To these meetings he and his wife went. He says, "They appeared humble, and their labors were abundantly blessed."

Mr. and Mrs. Henry gave in their names as seekers, and were admitted on probation. In speaking of the exercise of his mind at this time, he says, "I did not feel that all was well with me; that I had received the sealing evidence of God's Spirit, that I was a child of His in the strict sense of the word. I tried to attend to the means of grace, but could not feel that blessedness of which the saints spoke. In reading the Scriptures, I was often delighted with the contemplation of the goodness of God and His tender mercies towards man, and felt there was something enjoyed by Christians to which I was a stranger."

In this state of mind, he went to hear the Calvinistic Baptists preach; and he says the doctrines of election and foreordination there taught, were an *injury* rather than a *benefit* to him. Another untoward influence was brought to bear upon his mind at the same time, by a man by the name of Herred, who boarded with him. This man was a sceptic, and scepticism finds no stronger argument than is furnished by the doctrines of Calvinism. Without the support and enjoyment which an experimental knowledge of God can give, confused and bewildered by the conflicting doctrines of teachers who darken counsel by multitudes of words, he seems to have been driven to the verge of infidelity. His strong sense of right would not allow him to appropriate to himself a name and privilege to which he felt he had no claim. Accordingly he and his wife withdrew from the class, giving as their only reason, that they did not enjoy religion, and did not wish to deceive any one. Speaking of this, he says, "After taking this unwise step, I fell into many temptations and snares of the devil, and sinned against God, the best of beings, with a high hand and uplifted arm, until the year 1825."

All this time he continued to work on his farm, and was pushing ahead in his temporal affairs with all the energy of his strong and active nature.

In May, 1825, while on his way to attend court in Toronto, he fell in company with Elder Joseph Blackman, who was then a very young man. Like most of the first Christian preachers, he had " taken his life in his hand," and gone forth to preach the gospel, relying for support only on Him who feeds the ravens, and marks the sparrows fall. This young minister, with his kind and affable deportment, soon won his way to the stranger's heart; and Mr. Henry, after a little hesitation, told him the religious exercise of his mind. They had a long and interesting conversation together. Mr. Blackman told him he had an appointment near Port Oshawa, and invited him to attend. At that time Mr. Henry had never heard one of those people preach, who take only the name Christian, although A. C. Morrison had held some meetings in the vicinity. Mrs. Henry, however, who had retained more of her early religious feeling had been at some of the meetings, and heard both Balckman and Church speak. These men were full of zeal for doing good, and preached and exhorted with warmth and earnestness, alluding feelingly to the persecutions they had met with from the Methodists, who had obtained quite a footing in the township.

Mrs. Henry's sympathies were at once enlisted for these young strangers, while the gospel truths which they proclaimed found their way to her heart, and left an impression not easily worn off. She was almost continually repeating something these young men had said, and chiefly through her influence, he he was induced to attend the meeting.

Blackman preached, and at the close of the sermon

gave liberty to others to speak. Among those who availed themselves of this liberty, was a young man with whom Mr. Henry was acquainted, and who had been very wicked. He confessed his sins ; spoke of what the Lord had done for him, and fervently exhorted sinners to repent. This deeply impressed his mind. In the month of August he attended another meeeting held in a barn in Darlington. The Christians had no chapels in Canada then. Of this meeting, Mr. Henry says :

" J. T. Baily preached the Word with power; sinners wept; some cried aloud for mercy ; to me it was a solemn time. I went home wounded in spirit, for the Word of God cut like a two-edged sword, and I began to see myself as I was,—a poor lost sinner."

Mr. and Mrs. Henry both attended the next meeting, and together with Jesse Van Camp, afterwards Elder Van Camp, and his wife, at the close of the meeting arose and manifested a desire for prayers. After meeting the congregation repaired to the Lake Shore, and Baily baptized two happy converts by immersion. Of this meeting and his conversion, which followed, Mr. Henry tells us in the following simple, touching language : "It had a glorious effect not only in sealing former convictions, but in humbling the stoutest-hearted sinners. I saw Capt. John Trull bathed in tears, and made my way to him. He was my wife's uncle, and we had always been intimate friends. We took each other by the hand, and made a vow to seek God together. For about two weeks I sought the Lord with all my heart. I reflected much on the past, and deeply regretted that I had been so unwise and brought such a stain on the cause of Christ. The bitter pangs of self-reproach and the sorrow which oppressed my mind, caused me many wakeful hours. Sometimes I would try to pray in my family, but it only seemed to make me feel worse. Again I would retire to my barn or the grove, and pour out my soul to God. At times every sin of my past life seemed arrayed before my eyes; and Satan tempted me to believe that I had committed the 'unpardonable sin.' I searched the Scriptures carefully for light on this subject; and was much benefited by the perusal of a sermon by one Russell, a minister of the English Church. The gist of this sermon was, that there was no such thing as committing this sin, except where there was *light* in the head, and *malice* in the heart. He adduced the history of Paul, to show to what depths of sin a man may go, and yet be forgiven; also the example of Peter, who denied his Lord, to show that sin even against so great light may be forgiven, when there is no evil intent in the heart. This gave me courage to pray and ask for mercy, and for an evidence of my acceptance with God. About this time Elders Baily and Blackman came to make us a religious visit. In all my life, I had never before been visited by a minister of the Gospel. We invited in a couple of our neighbors also. They talked, and prayed, and sang with us, and urged us all to pray for ourselves. My mind had been much troubled on the subject of baptism, and I mentioned it to them. They said little about it, leaving it entirely with myself and God. Having been brought up under the traditions of the Episcopalians, baptism by immersion was something new to me. I had searched the Scriptures with great care, and also read a debate between Campbell and McCauly on the subject, and I already believed that immersion was baptism; but I was waiting—thinking of going forward, yet waiting for an evidence that God would accept me. The one great prayer of my heart was for an evidence of sins forgiven.

" On the 4th of Sept., 1825, I was at work alone in the field. I wept and prayed and again reviewed my past life: again my sins stood in dark array before me. My eyes were bathed in tears and my heart was ready to break; and there, alone in the field, I confessed my sins, and promised to obey God in all things. Bless His name! He not only humbled, but exalted me then and there! A great light broke into my mind; I forgot all my trouble, was strongly relieved of every burden and all distress, while my whole soul seemed full of bliss; my tongue was loosed, and I cried, 'Glory to God!' Then I sat down and asked myself what this meant. Was this religion? This the love of God shed abroad in the heart? Was this what I had heard Christians talk so much about? I was immediately impressed to go to the next meeting, and tell the exercise of my mind, and what the Lord had done for me."

The next Sabbath, Mr. Henry attended a meeting, held in a grove, where Elder Baily preached—standing in the shade of a maple tree, to a larger audience than could be accommodated in any building of which he could command the use. At the close of the sermon, Mr. Henry, his wife, and other young converts manifested a desire for baptism. The candidates, as was the custom of the time, were asked to relate their "experience;" and then a vote was taken to ascertain if it was satisfactory. There were a number of Baptist brethren present, who took part in the meeting, and were expected to vote.

Now Mr. Henry was not so fluent or so imaginative as some of the candidates, so his "experience" was not so satisfactory as theirs. If he could even have told a good dream, which was quite common on such occasions, it would have helped him in the estimation of the tribunal before which he stood; but as he could not, though the vote was unanimous in favor of his companions, a number voted against his being admitted to a participation in the ordinance. This would have discouraged one less in earnest, but Mr. Henry felt that it was a matter between him and God, not man, so he did not withdraw his request. Elder Baily then put the following questions to him: "Do you love God?" He answered, "Yes." "Do you love the people of God?" "Yes." "Have old things passed away?" "Yes; blessed be God." Elder Baily then concluded to baptize him. In spite of all his firmness, this lack of confidence on the part of those much older, and as he thought, much wiser and better than himself, had a depressing influence on Mr. Henry's mind. Nevertheless, he went forward in the discharge of duty, and was led down into the clear waters of Lake Ontario by the hand of Elder Baily, who little thought that the trembling convert, for whom he and his brethren entertained so many doubts and fears, was to become one of the strongest pillars of the Church. But so it was, and so it often is. In our religions, as in our physical life, the morning of brightest promise is overcast ere noon; while the dull cloud-obscured morning brings the brilliant day and glorious sunset. Making a profession of religion and being baptized was not a mere form with these sons and daughters of the forest; nor were the feelings and emotions under such bondage to the iron rules of conventional life as now. Becoming religious then meant a breaking up of the former modes of life—a cutting away from old moorings, and launching out on a new sea. This occasion was particularly solemn. The converts with faces bathed in tears, took leave of sinful friends and associates, exhorting them at the same time to flee from the "wrath to come."

A few days after this, Mr. Henry says, "I was sowing and harrowing in my fall wheat, but was all day engaged in prayer and meditation. My mind and affections appeared to be in heaven. Time passed swiftly while I was counting the cost of following Christ, or wrapt in anticipation of the joys of the blessed ones above. I have never known a happier day in my life." In the evening of that happy day, Mr. Henry attended a prayer and conference meeting held in a private house. At this meeting were present those friends who had refused to vote for his baptism. He was impressed to speak, he says, and tell the exercises of his mind. Those days of doubt and fear, those hours of sacred prayer and communion with God had not been in vain. The hour had come when his Father who seeth in secret, would reward him openly. He spoke; not in the rounded periods of the disciplined eloquence of the schools, but in the eloquence of a heart full of the Spirit of God, and overflowing with love for his saints, and aspirations for the salvation of sinners.

Ah, how should we, who have known Father Henry only in the full maturity of his powers, have rejoiced to have heard this first outburst of youthful religious fervor. No wonder those good brethren, who had so misunderstood the silent, diffident man, were startled as they listened, and recognizing in his words the language of the redeemed, come at the close of the meeting with tears in their eyes, to give him the right hand of fellowship. The good work continued to spread under the labors of Baily and Blackman.

From this time, Mr. Henry, instead of being doubted and distrusted, became a marked man among the converts, and many efforts were made to secure his membership in other churches. The Methodists and Baptists extended cordial invitations to him to cast his lot with them. But he sought a freer religious organization. He had taken his lessons in theology from God's own book, and not having there learned all those doctrines to which candidates for admission into these churches were expected to assent, he could not accept them. Unconditional election and its kindred doctrines, which had once so nearly driven him to infidelity, were particularly distasteful to him, as they are to all persons of generous, benevolent dispositions. Such never accept this dogma but under the pressure of early discipline. It must be instilled into their minds before fully developed or not at all. Close communion was another barrier between him and them. He felt that all God's dear children should meet together around their Father's table, irrespective of minor differences in belief. He had also learned from God's Book, that Jesus is the Christ, the Son of God, and accepted the sublime and life-giving truth in the earnest simplicity of his soul, and saw only mystery and confusion in the bewildering doctrines of the Trinity. However, there were in both of these churches, dear souls with whom he enjoyed sweet communion, and for whom he felt the strongest fellowship. Yet he chose to take God's Word alone for his guide, and cast his lot with the devoted few who were rallying around that standard.

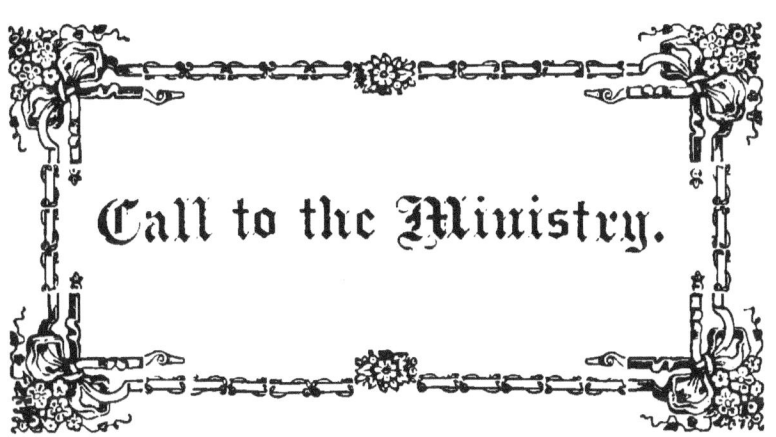

Call to the Ministry.

CHAPTER III.

CALL TO THE MINISTRY.

CONSIDERABLE interest in the religious welfare of this part of the Province of Ontario must have been felt by the Christian ministers of New York State at this time, as they were visited during this year, in addition to those already mentioned, by Elders T. McIntyre, J. Church, I. C. Goff, J. Blodget, and E. Shaw; the latter assisted Elder Baily in organizing a church in Darlington. Of this church, which numbered twenty-eight, Mr. Henry became a member. In the same place, and during the same month, September, 1825, was held the first Christian Conference in Ontario. J. T. Baily presided, and besides him were present J. Blackman and Isaac Goff, all young Christian ministers from United States. There were also present J. W. Sharrard, then a Baptist, afterwards a Christian minister, and Jesse Van Camp, Sisson Bradly, Wm. Noble, and Thomas Henry, besides a number of other persons. Thus Thomas Henry attended the first Session of the Canada Christian Conference, and never failed to attend a Session until 1879, when he died during its sitting in that year. Whoever else might be absent or present, all expected to see Eld. Henry, or Father Henry as he was called in later years, at his post.

That tender vine planted in the wilderness, and watered and tended with loving care by such faithful hearts, grew and brought forth fruit, until eighty souls were sheltered beneath its branches. During the long years which have passed away since those stirring times, that zealous band has been scattered, more by emigration than any other cause, and there is now no visible church in that place. The scattered branches, however, have not been lost, but have taken root in places to which they have been removed, and become centres around which other similar organizations have been gathered. Most prominent among these is the church in Oshawa, which is not more than ten miles from the original locality.

When we take into consideration that only inferior modes of travelling could be made available at that time to reach this part of Canada, that the country was new, and the people generally poor, and unable to offer any pecuniary inducement to visit them, we must conclude either that it was a point of special interest, or that the Christian ministers of that day were possessed of a more active missionary spirit than at the present time.

As we write these events our hearts swell with gratitude to God, and we cannot withhold a tribute of respect and veneration to those worthy laborers by whose self-sacrificing toil the standard of liberal Christianity was planted in these provinces. Most of them are gone from labor to reward. God give it to them more abundantly! As far as I know, only two of these laborers remain, Jesse Church and Isaac C. Goff. May the smile of heaven and the veneration of the brotherhood brighten their closing hours!

For the sake of our common Protestantism—I will not say Christianity, for that is always the same—I would rather not record some events which follow. Yet why should I hesitate? These are things of the past, and show by their contrast with the present liberal spirit among these denominations, and their general tendency to union, the progress they have made in the school of the Great Teacher, who prayed that all His followers might be one.

Mr. Henry soon found that the decision he had

made served to alienate the hearts of many professed friends, and brought upon him much unkindness and some persecution. This was trying to one so young in the cause; yet he met it with true Christian fortitude. Speaking of these things, he says: "I had taken the holy Bible, in the presence of God and men, to be my rule of faith and practice, and felt willing to suffer persecution rather than accept or teach for doctrines the commandments of men. I had become convinced that the great cause of division among Christians was their creeds and unscriptural terms. I therefore determined to speak of God only as He had revealed Himself in His sacred word; to apply to Jesus Christ only those titles given Him by His Father; to speak of angels and men, of baptism, and all other doctrines, in the language of the sacred volume."

Again, he says: "In the year 1827, I was called to pass through some severe trials of my faith, severe to me in my weakness and inexperience, though to others they may seem but trifles. About the first of January I went, in company with my wife, to attend a Methodist quarterly meeting, held in a school-house called Coryell's school-house, on the main road near Oshawa. Mr. Coryell and his wife, who lived near, were both members of the Christian denomination from New York; yet they had lodged four of the Methodist members, who came from a distance to attend the quarterly meeting.

"We reached the house in good season, and took our seats, thinking all was right. Mr. Brackenridge was presiding elder, Mr. Atwood circuit preacher, and Mr. Moore, a neighbor of mine, class-leader. I had great respect for Mr. Moore, also for Mr. Atwood, but knew the presiding elder to be a hard man. I soon perceived they were holding a council of war. Yes, it must have been a council of *war;* for it was not a council of *peace*. Presently I was called to the door, and questioned. Had I united with the Christians? I told them I had united with a people calling themselves only Christians. Did I believe in the Trinity? I told them I had never found that term in the Bible, consequently did not use it. I was then asked if I believed that Jesus Christ was the very and eternal God? I said, I believed Jesus was the Christ, the Son of God; that this was the belief of the Apostle Peter, and satisfied me. Again I was asked if I believed that the Father, the Son, and the Holy Ghost were one? I answered, Yes; not one in person, but one in work, one in testimony, and one in spirit. I told them I wished to be distinctly understood on this point, that one did not always mean one person. Paul and Apollos were said to be one. The three thousand who believed were one, and Jesus prayed that His disciples might *all be one*, even as He and His Father were one. These views, I told them, I honestly believed, and had come to their meeting only to get good. I was, however, told I must leave; such views could not be tolerated there. So I took my little wife, and went away. Others also left, among them Mr. and Mrs. Coryell, who lodged their members, and furnished the table and bread for their communion.

"I had my horses and sleigh with me, so we, the rejected ones, loaded up, and went to Darlington, where Eld. Baily was preaching in a private house. At the close of the sermon I arose, and repeated the whole circumstance. The relation had a great effect upon those who listened. They wept, and I cried. I felt, to say like one of old, 'If it had been from an enemy, I could have borne it;' but it came from ministers of the gospel, who profess to be called of God to preach deliverance to the captive, and the opening of prison doors to them that are bound."

This exhibition of a persecuting spirit resulted, as it usually does, in the advancement of the persecuted. It raised up new friends for them. Others had their eyes opened to the truth, and embraced the new doctrines; and in a short time fifty converts were baptized, and a church organized in the same house from which the few had been driven. This was the foundation of the Christian Church in Oshawa. Another circumstance, which occurred during the same year, left a lasting impression on his mind. He thus relates it:

"My father, at that time, kept a public-house at the Rouge, some twenty miles from where I lived. I was invited there to attend a wedding. Great preparations had been made for the occasion, as Archbishop Strachan was to perform the marriage ceremony. Taking advantage of the favorable opportunity, two children were to be brought to the house to be christened. The attendance at a public-house of the Archbishop of Upper Canada was quite an event, and it would be something for parents to tell, that the child was 'christened by the Archbishop.' To me the wedding had far less interest than the christening. It was the first time I had witnessed the ceremony since embracing scriptural views of baptism. According to the usual form, they chose godfathers and godmothers, who promised for their charges, first, 'That they should believe in God with all their hearts; second, That they should renounce the devil and his works; third, That they should keep God's holy will and commandments, and walk in the same all the days of their lives.' It affected me deeply to hear those solemn promises made by those who regarded them so lightly, as did the whole unscriptural ceremony. After performing the marriage ceremony and sprinkling the babes, a fiddler came in, and the whole company, with the exception of the Bishop, who had left, repaired to the ball-room. My father invited me to join the dance. I told him I could not conscientiously do so. To me it was sin, therefore I must be excused. The company were dancing over my head at the time. Father said, 'You cannot prevent the crows from flying over your head.' I replied, 'But I can prevent their making nests in my hair.'"

In 1828, Eld. Henry says, "The Methodists appeared more friendly. I had become acquainted with a local preacher, by the name of Cryderman, who was a good speaker, and appeared to be a very liberal man. I often went to hear him, and frequently spoke at his meetings. He invited me to attend a quarterly meeting which was to be held in Darlington, on the farm of Mr. Shaw, near the residence of the Hon. J. Simpson. I had a great anxiety to attend the meeting. I had a kind regard for the Methodists. I had begun to get over what they had done in Whitby, and really thought they would never do the same again.

I told him I would go. I saw the presiding elder, Mr. Courson, and told him Bro. Cryderman had kindly invited me to attend their quarterly meeting. He said he should be happy to see me there.

"So we dispensed with the prayer and conference meeting in the old school-house, from which we had once been driven, got a pair of horses and double waggon, collected a load of the young brethren and sisters, and went to the meeting. Others came on horseback. So we had quite a company. We arrived in good season for the Lovefeast. I saw that Bro. Cryderman was door-keeper, and took courage. To my surprise, as we approached Bro. Cryderman left the door, and Mr. Courson took his place. He at once asked me if we wished to go into the Lovefeast. I said it was for that purpose we had come. 'Well, Bro. Henry,' said he, 'we cannot let you in, unless you believe in the Trinity.' I told him I did not expect him to put such a question to me now; that I knew he had done so formerly, but thought he was becoming more liberal; and as I was invited to come, I had supposed I should be welcome. Then I told him, in the presence of them all, that he had no right to ask me, or any one else, that question, as neither Christ or His apostles required it of their followers. Then I said, 'Now, sir, I will remain outside; but would be pleased to have these young people, who have come so far, go into the Lovefeast.' He then passed around among them, as though it had been a class-meeting, asking questions something like the following. To a sister—

"'Daughter, you believe in the Holy Trinity?'

"'I never saw it in the Bible.'

"'My son, don't you believe that Jesus Christ is the very and eternal God?'

"'I always read, and believed, that Jesus was the Christ, the Son of God.'

"'You believe, my daughter, don't you, that three persons are one God?'

"'I believe, as it is revealed, that God is *one*.'

"By this time quite a company had collected around us, and the rev. gentleman, finding he was not gaining much ground, said he had not time to talk any more; but advised us, as it looked like rain, to go to a private house, and stay until after the Lovefeast, when we would be admitted. We chose to go to our waggon, and await the close of the *Lovefeast*, if such it might be called. At its close he came to us, and said to me—

"'How do you stand this? It will try you, and prove whether you are a Christian.'

"My reply was, 'Bro. Courson, I am surprised to hear you speak thus. I have yet to learn that God tries His children in this way. It is like tempting us, and it is written, "God tempts no man."' We went into the meeting. Mr. Courson, however, only injured his own cause. The best of his own members disapproved of his course, and our young brethren were more established in their principles."

If this chapter should come under the observation of any of our Methodist friends, we beg them to remember that these things occurred long ago, and that those were days of ignorance and prescription. We record this, and similar events, not as a reproach on the Methodists, but because they are part of the life of the man whose character we are delineating, and helped to form, as well as to exemplify that character.

These small things show, as the events of all his after-life do, a character at once strong and tender, firm and forgiving.

Mr. Henry had given up all for Christ; had offered soul and body a living sacrifice on the altar of his God. Much of his time was given to searching the Scriptures; much to self-examination and secret prayer. He also bore public testimony to the spiritual blessings which he enjoyed in secret, and spoke often of the goodness of God among his brethren. Those who listened to him, and were blessed by his warm exhortations, began to appreciate his gift; and he was called to take a prominent part in all their prayer and conference meetings. He too began to feel that hidden fire which burns in the soul of every true minister of Christ—that yearning over the souls of men, and that prophetic looking forward to their final destiny. But with these promptings came the overwhelming sense of the greatness of the work, and the bitter consciousness of his insufficiency. Like Moses, he exclaimed, "I am slow of speech." But, unlike Moses, he was not learned in all the wisdom of the Egyptians, or any other human school.

He deeply felt his need of education. But the still, small voice would not be silenced; day and night it followed him, whispering, "This is the way; walk in it. The church also appeared to hear the voice, at least they continued to put him forward, and in June, 1829, gave him letters recommending him as a public speaker. Eld. Jesse Van Camp, who had embraced religion, and been baptized at the same time, at the same time received letters for public improvement. A strong friendship existed between the two, and together they travelled and preached through the townships of Whitby, Darlington, Clarke, and Hope.

In Hope was a small church, composed of females, with the exception of one member—mostly young ladies; they kept up their meetings, and altogether maintained a sensible and exemplary deportment. The one male member did not long remain connected with the church; but the little band of females maintained their standing and influence until emigration, death, and marriage scattered them.

A part of Mr. Henry's labors were devoted to this church, and he formed an acquaintance with, and a fellowship for some of its members, which was not readily forgotten.

CHAPTER IV.

CLOUDS AND SUNSHINE.

HERE we pause in our record of the more public events of Mr. Henry's life, to paint a sorrowful domestic picture. Here we touch a cord which made every fibre of his great, strong heart vibrate to the touch of sorrow.

Mrs. Henry, who had united her destiny with his in his earliest manhood, and had thus far shared his holiest hopes and heaviest trials, was a very lovable woman. Being possessed of a pleasing person, engaging manners, and an amiable disposition, she was not only an object of deep affection in her own family, but beloved by all who knew her.

She was an excellent singer, and often would the notes of her bird-like voice awaken the echoes of the forest around her lonely home, or along the unfrequented roads by which she and her husband returned, sometimes late in the evening on horseback, from those little gatherings for public worship so common then. How little could her imagination picture then, what her home and the surrounding country have since became. Wonderful indeed have been the changes, but she is not forgotten. There are those who still cherish in the deepest recesses of their hearts, sweet remembrances of her short life of love and devotion. Still young in years, she and her husband had begun together that new and holier life, and might well look forward to many years of happiness in each other's society, and in the service of God.

As he had commenced the work of the ministry, and the deep responsibilities of that sacred office were beginning to gather around him, as well as the care of a growing family consisting of five sons, it is not strange they both felt that a great work lay before them. But the wise disposer of all events, who metes out to man the length of his days and the fulness of his years, changed all their calculations.

Mrs. Henry had a naturally delicate constitution, with consumptive tendency, and during the year of

1829 that insiduous disease commenced its ravages upon her frame.

Day by day it continued to sap the foundations of being, and drink at the fountain of life. Sometimes indeed there came days of seeming brightness, when the work of the destroyer appeared for the time to be stayed, and Hope ventured to whisper that she might still live. But all who are acquainted with that disease, know too well the meaning of such appearances. Life seems to linger a while as if in pity of our sorrow, and brighten with the semblance of health the frail tenement it is leaving; just as the sun lingers on the verge of winter, and gives us the bright days of Indian summer, as if loth to leave us without one kind farewell.

Much as she had to bind her to life, she seems to have been resigned to her fate; but her heart yearned sadly for the little ones she was leaving without a mother's care,—her five little boys. John, William, George, Thomas and Eben. She often exclaimed, "What will they do?" And he as often assured her the Lord would provide. She talked much with her husband about death and separation, and found in his courage, faith, and tenderness, the support and sympathy she so much needed. But her trust was in the loving Saviour. Oh, we never know how near

He can come to us until the days of suffering and weakness are upon us, and everything to which we cling seems sliding from our grasp.

In November, her husband took her and her youngest child, then about a year old, to visit her mother who lived twenty miles away, and returned home leaving them with her mother. While there a new phase of the disease was developed, which brought her to the verge of the grave in a few days. A hasty message brought her husband to her side, and all that under the circumstances could be done, was done to alleviate her sufferings; but the rude skill of the times was unavailing, as the most profound scientific knowledge would have been. They had to take her child away from her, and her husband went to carry it home. Oh, that long, lonely ride! Will he ever forget it? He went on horseback which was the easiest mode of travel over such roads, and took the little boy in his arms. The road lay mostly through the woods, with here and there a clearing and log-cabin by the way. Three times he stopped to get nourishment for the little one. Reached home in the gloom of twilight, gathered the boys around him, quieted them as best he could, went to a sleepless couch. In the morning he found some one to take care of the babe, and returned to his wife. The silent messenger had come in with noiseless step before him, and stilled the pulsations of the gentle heart, whose last throb was a prayer for his return. O could he have been beside her, and supported her head in the last hour, and gathered up the last broken sentences uttered by those dear lips, it would have been such a consolation to his grieving heart. The bright, sweet spirit was gone, and only the beautiful cold form was left to his embrace. O broken ties! O sad and sorrowing hearts! Were there no hereafter, no pitying Christ, no loving Father, what would you do?

They brought her home and the little boys looked on that saddest sight a child can see—the dead face of their mother. They buried her on that little eminence, where her babe and his mother already slept, near the shore of Lake Ontario, and the ceaseless murmur of the waves on the white pebbled beach, seems like a requiem to her memory.

The year which followed the death of his wife was one of great trial to Mr. Henry. He still felt it his duty to travel and preach, and the care of his family rested heavily on his mind. He did not then possess a great share of this world's goods, and in the new state of the country, the comforts and conveniences of life were hard to obtain.

An unmarried sister lived with him, and supplied as well as she could the place of the last one; but there was a great vacuum in his heart and life. He always found it difficult to live without sympathy. To the world he appeared strong and self-sustained; but away down in his heart was an unfathomable fountain of affection. Love was a part of his being, and he felt that he could not do his life-work nobly and well without the companionship of one true heart, which should abide next to his heart through sun and storm. Therefore at the end of the year, inclination as well as expediency pointed to another union.

He did not take this step without due deliberation, nor without the advice of his friends, as he felt that he had the interest of his family to look after, as well as his own. But he has told us about this matter, and we will repeat his own language :

"I counselled with my sister and friends on this important subject. I was well aware that a minister, and especially a widower was very closely watched. I did not wish to injure my character nor the cause of God; both were precious to me. I made up my mind that I would do my courting in a different manner from what it is generally done. I had formed some acquaintance with Miss Lurenda Abby, of the township of Hope. She was a member of that small church of females to whom I had preached occasionally. She had been at my place and seen my children, and I thought she was the one. So I concluded to write her a letter on the subject, and if she was agreeable, well, and if not, why that would be the end of it. Accordingly I wrote as follows:

"WHITBY, Oct. 10th, 1830.

"BELOVED SISTER,—

"I embrace this opportunity of writing to you for the first time, to let you know my mind. Since I first knew you, I have had for you, fellowship as a Christian, and respect as a woman. You no doubt have had trials and temptations, and cruel mockings from the enemy, but the Lord has been your refuge. He is a strong hold into which the righteous run and are safe. I too have known what afflictions are. I have suffered much persecution from the enemies of the Cross; but my greatest affliction has been the loss of my wife. Life since then has been a scene of sorrow and pain, and I am like the dove bereft of its tender mate. No one knows the trials through which I have passed. My children are without a mother's care, and I have no one into whose breast I can pour my complaints. This has led me to think much about seeking another companion, or help-meet—one who will care for my children, and bear the burdens of life with me.

"Having seen and formed something of an acquaintance with you, I have confidence in you as a Christian and as a woman. I would therefore ask, Do you feel disposed to unite in the holy bonds of matrimony; and if so, will you give me your hand; to live and die with me? I hope you will not take as an offence what I have written. Give me an answer as soon as possible. I have nothing more to say at present. 'I am your friend till death.'

"Thomas Henry.

"In a few days, to my great satisfaction, I received the following straightforward, sensible reply.

"Hope, Oct. 28th, 1830.

"Very Dear Brother,—

"After maturely weighing every circumstance relative to the subject of your letter, I can see no reasonable objection to the proposal with which you have been pleased to favor me. I am well aware of the very important duties that will devolve upon me in taking the place of a mother at so early an age. But looking to God, the great source of wisdom, for direction, and to you for counsel and advice, I shall endeavor to act with an eye single to the happiness and welfare of the family committed to my care.

"Having the fear of God continually before my eyes, I shall endeavor, with your assistance, to form their young minds for virtue's noble end, and to advance their eternal welfare by teaching them the fear of the Lord, and the first principles of our holy religion.

"With respect to ourselves, my dearest friend, you know that our happiness must greatly depend on our conduct towards each other; therefore, it will be our duty to strengthen each other's virtue, and reprove each other's faults with gentleness, and as much as in us lies, come up to that perfect standard of conjugal duty so admirably laid down by St. Paul.

"I should be happy to see you as soon as convenient, but if you cannot come soon, send a line the first opportunity.

"Yours affectionately. Farewell.

"LURENDA ABBY.

"At this time I was preaching occasionally in Hope, and soon made it convenient to call and see Miss

Abby, and make farther arrangements; and on the second day of Nov., 1830, we were married in Port Hope by an Episcopalian clergyman. The next day we started for home, and I soon had the pleasure of introducing to my children a mother of whom they have never had occasion to be ashamed. No one, who was not acquainted with the circumstances, would ever have known but what Lurenda was mother to the whole family. No difference has ever been made, but love and affection have ever existed between father, mother, and children. It was well understood that I should preach all I could, but I never intended to neglect my family as some ministers did; and I believe, I have always provided for my family. We were both very economical and industrious, and have always been blessed with enough of the good things of this life to make us comfortable, and to make our numerous friends comfortable when they visited us. God and the religion of Jesus Christ *first*, has always been our motto; all other matters were of minor importance, and must bow to the leading object of life."

No one who reads the foregoing will doubt Mr. Henry's being as fortunate in his second, as in his first choice. The second Mrs. Henry was an earnest active Christian; intelligent and well educated for the times, with a fine constitution and great energy and activity of character. If she was not more affectionate, she was stronger in body and mind, and well calculated to take up the cross, which the other had laid down in weakness; and bear it with honor to herself and family, through the busy years of a long life. She still lives in the old home. Though broken in health, and somewhat subdued in spirit, she is firm in her attachment to the cause to which her husband's life energies were devoted, consistent in her life, and always ready to welcome and entertain any of his numerous friends, who may call on her. Like her husband, she is, as far as I know, without an enemy; being one of the few ministers' wives who have come out of that trying position untouched·by the hand of jealousy or malice.

CHAPTER V.

EXTRACTS FROM JOURNAL—EARLY LABORS.

WE will here introduce some extracts from Mr. Henry's Journal.

"My father honestly thought I was in an error, and sent one Jackey Richardson to set me right on the doctrine of the Trinity, that first principle of the Christian Religion in their belief.

"He came one pleasant Sunday morning, and made known his errand. I told him I was thankful to my father for his care for my welfare, and also to him for his kindness in coming. Then I got the good old Bible and laid it on the table and said: 'Now sir, if it was not for this book, I should not know there was a God in heaven, any more than do the heathen. I should not know that man was a sinner, nor that Christ came to save such. Neither should I know how to obtain heaven. Having taken it as my only rule of religious faith and practice, I endeavor to observe the advice given by St. Peter: "If any man speak, let him speak as the oracles of God." The word Trinity not being found in the Bible, I do not use it.' After some more conversation, he took dinner with us and left, I hope thinking better of me than when he came.

"In 1830 a gentleman by the name of Jordan Post, who was present at a funeral where I preached, asked me to preach in his house, saying he had a large house with a commodious upper room which had been fitted up for a ball-room. I gave him an appointment, which I had to travel twenty-three miles on horseback to fill. This I did cheerfully, not for the hope of any earthly gain, but because, like Moses, I had an eye to the 'recompense of reward' away in the future; and because I loved my fellow-men, and wished to do them good.

"The congregation was large, many no doubt having come out of curiosity. One Methodist preacher was present and the class-leader, Jackey Richardson, of whom I have already spoken. The latter gentleman called me one side before the commencement of the meeting, and asked me if I believed as did one A. C. Morrison of the State of New York. I told him that I knew A. C. Morrison, and believed him to be a good man, and in good standing with one of the N. Y. C. Conferences, and that he had preached some in Canada to good acceptance. He said he had heard him, and that if I preached the same views he did, he would not stay to hear me. I advised him not to be hasty, but to stay and hear what I had to say; to prove all and hold fast what was good. He, however, left the room with his wife. On the way out he met a man named Secor coming in with his wife. Learning that he was leaving he remonstrated with him, telling him it was not right to judge of a thing without hearing. Richardson finally came back with him.

"I read a hymn, but could get no one to sing, so introduced the meeting by prayer. I then gave a short history of the rise of our people in the East, South, and West, where they came out all in one year, without any knowledge of each other; from the Baptist in the East, Methodist in the South, and Presbyterians in the West. I told them our people brought no creed with them but the Bible; no test of fellowship but Christian character; and no name but Christian. Finding I had got the attention of the people I named my text: 'But one thing is needful, and Mary has chosen that good part which shall never be taken from her.' From these words I endeavored to preach to them salvation through a crucified Christ and a risen Saviour, and had good liberty for one so timid. At the close I read another hymn, and all who could sing joined in singing it. I left another appointment and closed. My good brother Richardson came and shook hands with me, saying I had preached a good Methodist sermon. I said: 'Brother R., if I have preached the truth, give God the glory, and not Mr. Wesley.' There is a great wrong in this particular among the sects. When free salvation is preached, the Methodists claim it as their doctrine. When we preach Christian Baptism, the Baptists claim it as theirs. When we dwell on the influence of the Spirit, the Friends claim that, whereas all belong to God, and are parts of one harmonious whole."

In 1832, after much hesitancy and many doubts and misgivings on his part, Thomas Henry was ordained to the work of the ministry, in Darlington, Upper Canada — afterwards Canada West — now Ontario. The officiating ministers were T. McIntyre and Asahel Fish. The former preached the ordination sermon. Thus did Elder Henry, like many of the early ministers of this denomination, accept the great responsibility, and enter upon the sublime work of the **Christian Ministry**, with but little preparation except that made in communion with God and His Word. Unlearned in the wisdom of the schools, but strong in faith, and overflowing with fervor and love, they went into the world, bearing the cross of Christ through sunshine and storm, undaunted by opposition, and undiscouraged by disappointment. All honor to them! They were the men for the time and place. Little polished eloquence or profound logic was needed in the log-cabins of this then uncultivated country. The plain unvarnished truth, uttered with strength and sincerity, and sent home by the Spirit of God, did a great work and reached a class which a more disciplined ministry might have failed to affect. At all events, they did what they could in the great harvest where laborers were few.

The next four or five years after Elder Henry's ordination, were filled up by him without much variation, with work at home and ministerial labor. Though no lengthy record has been kept of these years, we have no reason to doubt that their work was faithfully done, as far as one pair of hands could do it. He says: "I never neglected my family, let circumstances be as they might." The consequence was, that he prospered in temporal as well as spiritual matters. The country improved, and property gained in value. With that wise foresight for which he was remarkable, he laid by each year a little, and as opportunity offered, invested his savings in land, which was then cheap, but rising rapidly in value. Thus he laid the foundation of competence for himself and family.

1834 was remarkable in the Oshawa church, for the beginning of that long and tedious controversy which arose between those who embraced the views of Alexander Campbell, and those who adhered to the original Christian platform. I do not intend to enter into the merits of the question at issue, nor pass an opinion on the conduct of either party. It is an episode in the history of the church, of which I can never think of with other feeling than that of profound sadness. Whatever may have been the motives of those who introduced these vexing questions, the result is deplorable, in that we have in Oshawa, and in other parts of Canada, two weak bodies of Christians, both professing to take the Bible alone for their creed, while neither is strong enough to make much headway against creeds and sectarianism. Had they remained together, as I believe a little more forbearance would have enabled them to have done, their influence for good might have been trebled. Speaking of this subject Elder Henry says: "I did not come out so hard on these brethren as some of our ministers did. I preached to both parties, and did all in my power to prevent a division, by kind words and gentle dealing; and in preaching always strove to give a 'Thus saith the Lord' for whatever I advanced."

At the annual meeting of the Conference in 1835 Elder Henry was appointed to superintend the drafting and circulation of a petition to the Provincial Parliament, that the Christians as a body might be known in law, or, in other words, have the same privileges enjoyed by other religious denominations. Until this time, and for years afterwards, the Christians were unable to solemnize marriages, or hold church property in the Province. This right was not, as in the United States, guaranteed to all religious bodies, but to certain denominations named. At first only the Established Church enjoyed the privilege, others obtaining it afterwards by petition. The Christians had more difficulty in obtaining this right than others, on account of the prejudice existing against United States, their first ministers having come from there. This being the case, they naturally made most converts among those who had emigrated from the States, or were natives of Canada. None of their ministers, and very few of the converts came from the Mother Country, or were educated there. To this day the

Christians form a liberal element in the population of the Provinces.

The petition was another responsibility, in addition to what Mr. Henry already had on his hands and heart. Still he continued to bestow much ministerial labor in Whitby, Pickering, Scarboro, and Darlington; sowing the good seed, watering the tender plants, and gathering in an occasional sheaf.

At the Conference in 1836 J. W. Sherrard—a man who had come from the Baptists—a man of education and influence, was ordained to the Christian ministry, and joined with Elder Henry in the effort for legal rights. Again Elder Henry writes:

"At the close of this Conference, I had put up at Bro. J. Ash's two miles below Cobourg, with a number of other brethren, when I was startled by the arrival of a messenger, who informed me that my father lay at the point of death—could not possibly live but a short time. I made my way home as soon as possible, and found him at my house nearly gone. He knew me, however, and asked me to pray for him. God only knows my feelings as I bowed by that bed of death. He died in a short time. Elder Van Camp preached at his funeral, which was attended by a large concourse of friends and relatives. His remains were deposited by the side of mother's, and near his other relatives in the family burying-ground on the hill beside the lake."

This year Elder Henry attended the N. Y. W. Conference held at Shelby, and received a flattering testimonial from them. He had previously attended several sessions of the N. Y. C. Conference, and formed many pleasant acquaintances there. He always loved these gatherings of his brethren.

The Rebellion.

CHAPTER VI.

THE REBELLION.

THE years of 1837-8 were eventful years in the history of Canada; it was during those years that the Rebellion took place. It is not our province to give an opinion of the political merits of that convulsion, which shook the country throughout its length and breadth. We may, however, suggest that it was one of those outbreaks, which are apt to follow long periods of misrule, in countries where the people have no legal means of redress. A sad struggle it was, and unfortunate in many respects; yet it opened the eyes of men in power, and was the means of securing many privileges to the inhabitants, and breaking up the monopoly of the Family Compact. Religious organizations, as they usually do in times of political disturbance, suffered; and the Christians, from the same causes which operated against their political recognition, suffered more than others; their members were subject to unjust suspicion, which caused much annoyance. Many of them left the country, and some of the smaller churches lost their visibility. Elder Henry speaks of this period as follows:

"The years of the Rebellion will never be forgotten by me. We suffered much on account of our liberal views, and peace principles. I was well acquainted with Wm. Lyon McKenzie: he was a staunch reformer and friend to his country. At the commencement of the disturbance he published a paper in Toronto. On account of his liberal views, and some exposures of the Family Compact, he was beset by a mob of their sons, and, I am sorry to say, a son of Archbishop Strachan was among them. They came in the night, broke open his office, and threw his type and press into the lake; but his friends soon got him another press and more type. This cruel act served to bring him before the public, and he was elected member of Parliament. I supported him from principle. I was well acquainted with Lount and Matthews, and stood near when they were executed at Toronto as leaders of the Rebellion. I was a witness for Dr. Hunter when he was tried for treason, and the foreman of the jury told me afterwards it was my evidence that saved him. Having been at his house on the evening of the fight in Toronto, I was able to clear him from being there. I was not only a friend to British law and to order, but I had much sympathy for many who unwisely took up arms against it."

That is what Mr. Henry says of himself in connection with the Rebellion, but he does not record, and probably at the time it would not have been safe to record, the many deeds of kindness and Christian charity, performed on behalf of those unfortunate men, who upon the suppression of the outbreak became outlaws and outcasts from home. His house was a refuge and safe asylum for them. Being a native of Ireland, and having taken no active part in the disturbance, he was comparatively free from suspicion. His house, barn, and even cellar, were often occupied by those who dared not be seen abroad; here they were concealed, fed, and comforted, until an opportunity could be found for them to cross the lake, and take refuge on Republican soil. More than once, his sons and his team met the lonely wanderers at appointed places along the shore of the marsh or lake, and brought them to a safe retreat. And again have the same agents conveyed them to out of the way places, where they could embark on some American vessel bound for the " other side."

Many of these incidents were interesting and some quite exciting. John, the eldest son, a wide awake youth of seventeen, the principal actor on such occasions, was in his element; had he been older he might, in spite of parental advice, have been among the agitators.

At one time, about a dozen refugees were concealed in a house some three miles from Oshawa Harbor. Somebody gave John to understand that his services were needed in that direction on a particular night. Without his father's knowledge, he took the team, put all the bells on the horses he could get, drove to the place, got the men in the sleigh, drove back through Oshawa about midnight, and had his men on board a schooner before daylight without molestation; when if he had gone quietly, he would have been suspected, and probably arrested. The schooner was waiting for them in the marsh, that stretches back from the lake at Port Oshawa.

One night after the family had retired, Dr. Hunter, of whom we have spoken, presented himself at Elder Henry's door. He was cautiously admitted, and soon told his trouble in hurried whispers. Fresh evidence of his disloyalty had been obtained, and the officers of the law were on his track. Elder Henry well knew he could do nothing for him outside of the house without awakening suspicion. He therefore conducted him to the room where his sons were in bed. John took in the situation at once, and in an incredibly short time was dressed, and had left the house with the medical man, who dared not remain there an hour. They crossed the fields like two shadows, and were soon lost to sight in the wood skirting the marsh. John was familiar with every nook and tree of that wood, and guided the doctor by a circuitous route to a shanty on the border of the marsh, where an old man lived alone. The doctor was soon disposed of in bed, and as it was some time until daylight, the young man sat down to think. It was the latter part of March, and considerable ice was still in the marsh. A vessel that had wintered there was being prepared for sailing. The captain and owner of the vessel, Jesse Trull, was John's uncle, and though he dared not make his business known to his uncle, the relationship would furnish him an excuse for being there. He knew his uncle to be favorably disposed to his cause, yet he felt that he would not risk concealing a refugee on his vessel, which would be thereby subject to confiscation. But the mate, an eccentric man called Billy Barrow, he knew he could depend on for assistance. When daylight came, John went down to the boat, but there a new danger presented itself. Sergeant Martin, a government officer, had been stationed there on purpose to keep refugees from going on board. With a quickness of perception and promptness of action, remarkable in one of his age, the youth took of his coat, and went to work with the men, who were clearing away the ice from around the boat. He was soon accosted by Sergeant Martin, who demanded what he was doing there.

"Helping my uncle get his boat off!" was the ready answer.

He worked all day, took his meals with the crew on board, and at night went to the cabin with Billy Barrow. Mr. Trull did not stay on board at night, so the two had the cabin to themselves. They had little chance of communication during the day, but they now talked the matter over in whispers, and laid their plans for Hunter's escape. When all others were asleep, John stole away to the shanty, carrying supplies to his man, and reporting progress. There was another morning, another challenge from Sergeant Martin, and another day's work for John. They had hoped to get the boat ready to sail that day, but night came, and it was evident the programme of the last two days was to be repeated.

That night, when John went to carry supplies to

his man, he went farther ; and before his return a little red skiff was snugly concealed behind a point nearly a half-mile west from the harbor. The third day drew to a close, and the schooner was free from the ice, and floated out into open water, ready to sail in the morning, as soon as she could obtain a " clearance."

Between 12 and 1 o'clock that night, two figures instead of one emerged from the shanty, and proceeded cautiously towards the point where the red skiff was concealed. It was a wild, dark night, but the young man's accustomed feet led the way, and the doctor followed with nervous tread. They reached their destination safely, and found the skiff where he had left it. They looked out over the water, and for a moment stood silent, almost irresolute. It was a fearful venture. The wind was blowing almost a gale, breaking the water into yeasty waves, mixed with fragments of floating ice. The case was urgent. The dauntless young man launched his boat among the seething waves, and ordered the doctor to lie flat in the bottom ; for the boat was barely safe for two on calm waters, and he knew that with his unaccustomed companion erect in it, they would surely be swamped. The gentleman at first demurred at this arrangement, but being bluntly informed that he must obey orders or he would be left to look after himself, submitted ;

and the frail craft was soon tossing among the breakers. Clouds of inky blackness enveloped the sky, and entirely hid the schooner from their view, but the intrepid oarsman held on his way, steering half by guess, until a fiercer gust of wind made a rift in the clouds, and gave him a glimpse of the masts of the vessel, towards which he steered. As they passed the outlet of the marsh, cakes of ice were floating seaward, and a large piece came in contact with the little skiff, threatening to capsize it. The doctor made a move to rise, but an assurance from John, that a blow from his oar would quiet him if he did not keep quiet, caused him to lie still, until they drew up on the lee-ward side of the vessel, and the little red skiff was made fast to a rope, which John knew would be hanging in a convenient place near the stern of the boat. Shortly after this, two dark figures might have been seen climbing into the schooner, if any one had been there to see them. As it was, only the wind and waves were around them, and the dark clouds above. They stood on the stern deck, and a dark hole, just about large enough to admit a man's body, was before them. This led down into a small dark place only a few feet square, where odds and ends which it was desirable to have out of sight, were usually thrown. Billy Barrow had prepared this place for their passenger. John taking his hand helped him lower himself into his snug quarters, and then putting on the "hatch," was soon after in the berth with the mate, to whom he dared to communicate his success only by a *nudge*, which was answered in the same way. After waiting until certain that no one had been disturbed, Billy Barrow crept softly on deck, and proceeded to put large bolts into the corners of the "hatch," in holes previously bored for them ; to give it an appearance of great security. Then he closed the cracks with oakum and pitch, having previously prepared a place for ventilation from the freight room.

In the morning all was activity on board the boat. About nine o'clock, John Trull, Militia Captain, and brother to the boat owner, came on board to search the vessel. The duty was strictly performed, but as no contraband goods or men were found, the captain got his " clearance ;" landsmen came ashore, the schooner weighed anchor, and sailed away with Dr. Hunter towards the " other side." We know nothing more of his adventure, than that he reached the Republic in safety.

Again Elder Henry says : " I was much engaged in preaching at that time, and was called to preach some funeral sermons that were a trial to me, and I fear little comfort to surviving friends. Among these was that of one Thomas Conat, who was killed instantly by a blow from the sword of a dragoon in government employ; he was under the influence of liquor at the time, and probably said something insulting to the soldier. Another was that of a young man by the name of McCall, who was stabbed with a butcher knife by one Skinner, who was afterwards hanged for the deed. Skinner lived at the time, not far from me, and his wife was sick, and family in such destitute circumstances that I was obliged to take my horse and sleigh, and go out among the farmers and gather up provisions for them. Soon after I was called upon to preach the funeral sermon of a man who had shot himself; and in a short time again, for one who had committed suicide by cutting his throat. This last case was particularly trying to me. The family were respectable. His son asked me if I would come and preach a funeral sermon for his father. I felt for them, but hardly knew what to say to comfort them. When I arrived at the school-house in Bowmanville, where meetings were frequently held—as Churches were scarce in those days, I found a large congregation assembled, and felt that something must be said. I told them my mission was to preach to the *living* not to the *dead*. So I took a text and preached as well as I could, warning all to prepare to meet God. To the mourning widow and children I said, the good Father would not forsake in this hour of sad bereavement, if they put their trust in Him."

Pastor at Oshawa.

CHAPTER VII.

PASTOR OF OSHAWA CHRISTIAN CHURCH.

ABOUT the commencement of 1839 the political disturbance had in a great measure subsided, but its effect remained in the low state of public morals, and general declension of the churches. From causes before mentioned, none had suffered more than the Christians. The following extract from a letter written by Elder Henry to J. Badger, editor of the *Christian Palladium,* presents as clear a picture of the existing state of things as can well be given in so many words.

"The rebellion has been very much against us, as it has caused many of our preachers to leave this country for the States. Besides this, a great many of our brethren do not believe in fighting at all with carnal weapons; therefore certain persons whose loyalty is a trade, have represented that we were disaffected to the Government; thereby preventing us from obtaining our legal rights. A few days since Elder Sharrard and myself went to Toronto to make some enquiries about our petition, which has passed the third reading in the Lower House. We went to Mr. Sullivan, one of the Governor's Council. Having made our business known, we were asked a great many questions, which we answered; and told him we were ready to answer more, if he had them to ask.

"He told us that if Canada remained a British Province, all American teachers and preachers would be prevented from settling in it, and then we should dwindle away and come to nought; he therefore considered it best not to be in a hurry about granting our request. Thus you see we have our own difficulties to contend with. I do hope you, or O. E. Morrill, or both of you, will try to attend our next Conference, for if we ever needed help it is now."

The Session of Conference, to which Elder Henry referred, was held in Whitby, and Elder Badger, who appears to have been a friend in need, attended.

Elder Henry was again called to preside, and he speaks of it as a good and profitable time.

In 1840 Elder Henry was chosen to the pastorate of the church in Whitby, since called the Oshawa Christian Church. Oshawa is a village in the township of Whitby, and takes its name from Oshawa Creek, on which it is located. Oshawa signifies in the Indian dialect, White Fish, or White Fish Creek, and formerly abounded in white fish; and Elder Henry could tell some exciting tales of early exploits, in fishing in its waters.

To return to our subject, Elder Henry had long been pastor of the churches in Darlington, Clarke, and Scarborough. The Oshawa church was at first considered a branch of the church in Darlington, but was afterwards organized into a separate church. At this time it was in a very unhappy condition. The wearing controversy on Mr. Campbell's theories, still continued unabated. Elder McIntyre, its former pastor, had left, and it was almost impossible for the warring elements to agree on a man to fill his place. Elder Henry had all the time kept the confidence of both parties, and was finally chosen unanimously to fill the position; and he was probably the only minister on whom they could have agreed. His conduct was conciliatory, and in his sermons he avoided extremes, and dwelt on those points on which all could agree.

The early Christian ministers conscientiously refused to accept stated salaries, living on voluntary contributions from the brethren, or supported themselves by the labor of their hands. When Elder Henry was chosen to this responsible position, it was without the expectation or promise of any reward, save what was to be found in doing good. In speaking of those times he says, "More work was done then for love and the good of souls than is now done for salaries." It is doubtful if Elder Henry has *ever* received as much from the churches as would defray his travelling expenses.

Under date of April, 1841, he writes:

"Brother Marsh, my only apology for not writing sooner is the want of time. My business is crowding, and calls for the preaching of a free gospel are abundant. Since I wrote you last we have had many precious seasons here. My preaching for the past winter has been confined mostly to Whitby and Darlington. In the month of March I baptized twenty-three happy converts, and three of the number were my own sons. This has given me great joy.

"T. Henry."

The years which immediately followed Elder Henry's appointment to the pastorate of the Oshawa Christian Church, were years of upward progress and general prosperity. A brighter day had dawned both on the church and country. The earnest, energetic spirit of the pastor was infused into his flock. They began to feel an interest in the work before them, and an inclination to contribute of their means for its advancement. The necessity of a suitable house for the worship of God had long been evident, and the work was commenced. It is hardly necessary to add that Elder Henry was the life and soul of this enterprise. Though receiving no salary for his labors as pastor, he nevertheless contributed of his means, and gave much of his time and labor to the work. It was a success. The chapel was finished, and was large and expensive for the times, and spoke well for the liberality of the churches. We should naturally suppose that Elder Henry during these years found employment for head, hands and heart in the work at Oshawa, but no one vicinity could monopolize these. His heart yearned over all the vineyard, and he went frequently among the other churches; always arousing, encouraging, and comforting as he went; and seldom failing to gather a few clusters for the Master by the way. He was then in the full vigor and strength of his manhood, and his labors were almost gigantic. Could he, during those years, have devoted more time to self-culture his usefulness in after life would have been enhanced. He deeply felt this, but saw no time for study. The requirements of the season were pressing, and he did his heaviest day of work where and when it was most needed; and the recording angel has written it down in that great ledger, where all accounts are justly balanced.

The sun does not shine always on the same fields. Rain fell in the midst of harvest. The long fermenting questions which vexed the church, assumed a definite form, and the wearisome discussions culminated in a division of the body. Those brethren who advocated the views entertained by A. Campbell withdrew, and formed a separate church, known as the Disciples of Christ.

Elder Henry remained on the old platform, and without wasting time in vain regrets, applied himself at once to the work of rebuilding the walls, and healing the wounds of Zion.

The following letter written for, and published in the *Palladium* is characteristic:

"Brother Marsh, our Conference met in Newmarket. We had a good time. The visit of Elders

McIntyre, Marvin, and Galloway, was like the coming of Titus. They attended a general meeting in Whitby, which was truly an interesting season, and one long to be remembered. On the 16th and 17th I attended a meeting in Haldimand with Elders McIntyre and Marvin; Elder McIntyre baptized two. We feel much encouraged. Since Conference I have baptized sixteen happy converts. I have attended a number of meetings this season in Whitechurch with Elder Sharrard. We have baptized nineteen in a beautiful little sheet of water called Mussulman's Lake. The work is progressing. I have just returned from a visit to the State of New York, in company with my wife, and Deacon J. Ainsbury and wife. At Marion I attended a two days' meeting. From Marion went to Auburn, and spent a day visiting the State Prison and prisoners. We returned home by way of Niagara Falls, and spent two days there visiting some friends, and viewing that wonderful work of God, the great cataract. From here we made our way to Lewiston, and took the steamboat across our own beautiful lake to Toronto; reached home the following evening and found all well.

"T. HENRY."

Again in October we find another letter in which he gives an account of attending a meeting in Whitechurch, and baptizing 12, with prospects still flattering; but closes with the remark that good and wise shepherds are needed to feed the flock. We cannot but notice in his writings this constant appeal for help. The vastness of the work, and the scarcity of laborers was ever present to his mind.

On the 28th of May, 1843, the new chapel was opened, and dedicated to the worship of God, and the promotion of liberal Christianity.

Elder J. Badger preached the dedicatory sermon. Mr. Henry wrote: "I regard it as one of Badger's best efforts. A number of our ministers were present, all of whom took part in the exercises. The chapel is 54x38 feet, has a gallery on three sides, is well painted, and cost $2,450. The day was pleasant, and it was thought 400 had to leave for want of room. On the 8th, 9th and 10th of July, a General Meeting and the Session of the Canada Christian Conference was held in the new chapel, and Elder Henry again called to preside.

We can scarcely fashion the figures which stand for eighteen hundred and forty-three without recurring mentally to the memorable religious excitement connected with that year, growing out of Mr. Miller's then new exposition of prophecy. The influx of members to the churches was very great; and no doubt some good fruit-laden sheaves were gathered in. Yet when we read of the numerous conversions and baptisms of that period, we look in vain for the strong and extensive churches in which they should have resulted, and are forced to the conclusion, that many who flocked to the sheltering fold were driven there from fear of a near-approaching storm, rather than from love to God or sympathy with His people. In this may be seen the wisdom of the great Disposer of events, in keeping the times and seasons in His own hand. Elder Henry, firm as he was true, was not carried away by the general excitement, though we have no reason to suppose that he loved the appearing of the Saviour less than those who were swept along by the general inundation of feeling. He did not, however, as some did, oppose the movement by harsh deeds and harsher words, but gently and cautiously advised those around him to watch and wait. By his prudence, forbearance and ready sympathy with whatever was good in the movement, he was able to gather all that was of real value which the swollen waters brought within his reach, and at the same time preserve his flock from much of the evil which followed the receding tide. During the year he baptized 150 converts. In the month of

April alone 123. In May he attended a meeting in Mariposa, and administered the communion to a large number, more than half of whom were Methodists In the three years of his pastorate, he had seen the membership of the church of his charge raised from 28 to 174. Few men are as well calculated for the pastor's office as was Elder Henry. In the first place, having the cause at heart made him thoroughly in earnest. Active and energetic in whatever he undertook, and punctual to the moment, things never lagged behind where he led. Having a remarkable faculty for remembering details, small matters were not likely to be neglected.

He had also an ability for making himself at home in the house of God, and making others feel the same, thereby divesting worship of that stiffness and distance from the heart and life which destroys much of its power.

Having a quick sympathy with the common joys, sorrows and needs of humanity, and an ability of adapting himself to circumstances, he was an efficient as well as welcome visitor. I have known him to make as many as fourteen calls in a day, finding time at each place to say something to cheer and benefit those he visited, make a favorable impression himself, and say a few words for his Master. He had not, as some ministers are accused of having, a beaten path to the houses of the wealthy. The poor, the sick, the ignorant and disagreeable were remembered, and every one made to feel that he or she was of some consequence, and had a part in the work. He was also fond of social gatherings, and no anniversary, tea-meeting, or donation was complete without Elder Henry.

Elder Henry's youngest brother—Elder William Henry, the only surviving member of his family, is also a minister of the Christian denomination. He lives in Harriston, Ontario, and though not so widely known as Thomas, has many of his characteristics. He embraced religion among the Methodists, and was for a number of years a member of that body, though now loyal in sentiment and life to the Christians, he retains much of the fervor of the people with whom his early religious life was spent. Like his brother, he is active and business-like in his habits, and earnestly devoted to the cause of liberal Christianity.

CHAPTER VIII.

THE LUMINARY—LEGAL RECOGNITION—LOSS OF FRIENDS.
A LETTER.

THE years that followed the exciting period of 1843, were a season of comparative quiet in the life of Eld. Henry, and in the churches of Canada. Eld. Langdon had been employed to preach in Oshawa, but Eld. Henry was still the pastor, and preached part of the time there, and went about more among the churches where his coming was always welcomed with joy. More laborers were now in the vineyard, and he had oftener than formerly the privilege of greeting loved co-workers in the cause he so dearly loved.

At the Conference in 1844, the propriety of publishing a denominational paper in Canada was discussed.

In a letter to the *Palladium,* dated Nov. 29th, Eld. Henry writes:

"We hope the *Christian Palladium* will still be taken and read by many in Canada, and that harmony and friendly co-operation may exist as heretofore. Though the *Palladium* is conducted by good and able men, yet it does not in all respects meet our wants in Canada. The printing press is purchased, and the paper will go on, conducted by Eld. Wm. Nobles and Mr. Hicks; I am not without fears respecting this enterprise."

The *Christian Luminary* was published at Oshawa, and was both a convenience and satisfaction to the Canadian Churches; but the result proved that his fears were well grounded. The Christian membership was too small in the Province to justify the undertaking. Considerable enthusiasm was manifested in its support, but it was never a paying enterprise. It finally fell into Eld. Henry's hands, as burdens generally did, and he continued its publication at a sacrifice until 1849, when it was discontinued.

In 1845 Eld. Henry writes: "This has been a marked year in my life. Our cup is a mixed one. We may have joy in the morning, but sorrow cometh in the evening. In the first part of February I was moved to visit my brothers who lived near Guelph. I started accordingly, accompanied by my wife. The snow was deep, and we had an uncommonly hard journey. When within about three miles of the place we met my brother William. Being very tired we were overjoyed at the meeting, but soon, alas, our joy was turned to sorrow, for he informed us that my dear brother James was dead. He had died the day before of inflammation of the lungs, and we had arrived in time to attend the funeral, which was to take place at two o'clock the next day. We had expected to meet him well and happy, and enjoy a pleasant visit with him. We arrived at his house and found him cold in death, with his wife and nine children weeping around him. It was an affecting time. The next day about eighty sleighs filled with people met at the house, and followed his remains to the Manse burying ground."

We find in the *Luminary* of March, 1845, the following announcement:

"I have the gratification of announcing to our friends, that I have just received a letter from Mr. T. Williams, M.P., stating that his Excellency, the Governor-General, on the 17th ult., came down in state to the honorable the Legislative, and assented in her Majesty's name to the Bill presented by him to the Legislature in our behalf.

"T. Henry."

Thus after so many years of waiting and working, the Christians in Canada obtained that political recognition necessary to their prosperity as a religious body. No one had worked so hard or done so much towards the accomplishment of this object as Mr. Henry. He had circulated the petitions, had visited Montreal and Quebec and Toronto in pursuance of this object, and now felt that he was rewarded for his labor.

During the next three years, much of Eld. Henry's time, and a great deal of thought besides considerable money, were devoted to the support of the *Luminary*. He was doubtful from the first of the expediency of the undertaking, yet no one worked so hard, or sacrificed so much as he did in its behalf.

In Sept., 1846, Eld. Henry's second son, Wm. Henry, died, after an illness of five days. He was an intelligent, upright young man, and one of the three whom Eld. Henry mentions as having been among the number he baptized in 1841. He conversed freely with his father and friends about his departure, and expressed his confidence in Christ, and his hope of a glorious resurrection. He was not only loved and highly prized in the family, but respected and valued by all who knew him. But at the early age of 24,

> "He who young and strong has cherished
> Ardent longings for the strife,
> By the way side fell and perished—
> Weary with the march of life."

Extracts from Eld. Henry's letters for the *Luminary* in 1847, will show that he still enjoyed visiting conferences and churches abroad, and felt a deep interest in their prosperity. "I have just returned from attending the N. Y. Eastern and Western Conferences, which were seasons of great interest. How pleasant are these reunions of ministers and brethren after a year of toil and care. They are like the green spots which the traveller meets in his journey across the desert, and we always go out from them rested and refreshed."

Again. "Our Conference and General Meeting in Cramahe were of deep interest. All matters of difference were amicably adjusted, and our meeting and visit there were of an encouraging nature."

"On Saturday and Sunday the 4th and 5th inst., I attended a meeting in the Newmarket C. Chapel.

It was a good meeting, and the brethren and sisters spoke freely of the goodness of God. It was remarked by one of the brethren, that they did not know how much they loved each other until they were separated. The church has had a good revival."

In 1848-49 in addition to acting as publishing agent for the *Luminary*, Eld. Henry with the assistance of Eld. Geo. Colston published a Hymn Book. He writes in the *Luminary:*

"I would say to our patrons, that we have commenced publishing the Hymn Book, of which we spoke in a previous number, and our expenses are greatly increased; we therefore call on them to send us what is due on former volumes. We expect to have it completed in September. Let there be a united effort to enable us to carry on the Book and *Luminary* both. We were expecting some of our wealthy brethren would come forward and assist us in publishing the Hymn Book, but we find it is easier to get into a hard spot than to get out."

The Hymn Book was finished, and the edition all sold; but as another edition was never published it fell into disuse, and the churches in Canada have since been supplied with books from United States. There are, however, some of our old brethren and sisters who cling to our Canadian Hymn Book ; and as late as 1878 Eld. Henry had an application for one. At the close of 1849 the *Luminary* was discontinued, and its list handed over to the *Christian Palladium.*

During the years 1850, 51 and 52, Eld. Henry gave less time to the work of the ministry than at any other period since his ordination. He was one of the stockholders of the Oshawa Harbor Company, and as the Harbor Master had died of cholera, and things were in an unsatisfactory state, he was induced at the urgent request of the other stockholders to accept the position of Harbor Master. He filled the position with credit to himself, and to the satisfaction of all concerned. He however remained pastor of the Oshawa Church, and never lost his interest in it, or in the cause to which his life had been devoted. He writes to the *Palladium :* " As for myself I am not doing so much in the cause as in former years, yet, bless God, I love His holy name, and love to preach the unsearchable riches of Christ. " The Oshawa Church usually had the services of some other minister two or three Sabbaths in the month, but their faithful old pastor preached as often, at least, as once in a month, administered the communion, attended Church meetings and had the general oversight of things.

In addition to Father Henry's other labors he always carried on an extensive correspondence. Few men have written more letters, besides numerous short articles contributed to our various denominational periodicals, in which he evinced a great capability for gathering interesting items of useful intelligence, and aptness in communicating. He wrote a great number of private letters; letters on business, letters of friendship, letters of advice, letters of condolence and letters of congratulation. Some of these letters are among the best things he has ever written, but we have not many in our possession as they were not often copied.

The following epistle is characteristic:

"Dear Sister Bartlett:

"Since you were here last I have thought of you a great many times. I deeply sympathise with you in your affliction, and have been thinking I would write you a letter, and express my feelings to you, perhaps for the last time. I have never forgotten, nor can I ever forget your kindness to me and my family in our great affliction; and gratitude as well as sympathy prompts me to ask if I cannot offer a word that will comfort you, by drawing a contrast between the sorrows of earth, and the joys of heaven.

How transient are the joys of earth! Yesterday they seemed almost complete. To-day they have utterly failed us, and the soul is left sorrowful, as if hope and smiles had never been. Yesterday was all sunshine ; to-day is all darkness. Yesterday a home sheltered us; to-day we have ashes instead. Yesterday a little child sat on our knee ; to-day we sing a funeral dirge, and lay it in the tomb.

Such are the joys, the hopes, the treasures of earth. This moment they are, the next they are gone, and we are left alone and helpless. Hard as this may seem, it is as God, our Father, would have it. It is his own Providence. He would thus wean us from earth, thus turn our steps towards heaven, and not back to our former bondage.

" If with all this life's disappointment we love it too much, how much more we should cling to it, if prosperity always attended our steps. God knows what is best, and doeth all things well. We are compensated for all our present ills, by that which is unseen— which is ours by faith, and not by sight. If earthly bliss is transient—heavenly bliss is eternal. Dear sister in Christ, look up! If faithful, we shall soon be in the promised land. Soon be beyond the reach of tears and anguish. Not a sigh, or tear, or note of grief shall ever be heard or known in that glorious habitation—that house not made with hands. For such a life, for a bliss so pure, let us run with faith, endure with patience, and keep our eye fixed on the rising towers, the streets of gold, and the river of life —the New Jerusalem—and what a meeting will be there! Such an one as was never known in earth's happiest home, or holiest sanctuary. The good of all ages will be there. The Babe of Bethlehem, the Christ who wore the thorny crown, will be there. And the presence of the Great I Am will light the Holy City, whose beauty never fades, and whose crystal stream flows on forever.

"Oh, shall not this glorious prospect enable us to bear the trials of this life with patience, and bow in cheerful submission to the will of our Father who has prepared such glorious things for us.

"As ever, your Brother in Christ,

"T. Henry."

CHAPTER IX.

MISSIONARY WORK—RESIGNS PASTORATE.

IN 1853 Elder Henry was appointed Home Missionary, to travel throughout the bounds of the Conference. The following extracts from his report will show how his time was occupied.

"Dec. 4.—Attended fellowship meeting in Oshawa; had a good meeting; and next day preached and baptized three. On the 7th, pursued my way to Haldimand. Preached twice on Sabbath; obtained twelve members for the Missionary Society, and collected £1 2s. 6d. Visited the church in Cramahe. They have promised to make a donation in aid of the Mission. 18th.—Preached near Port Credit in the forenoon, and in the afternoon near Oakville. Spent a little time visiting the brethren, and collected £2. On Christmas preached to the church in Waterloo, in company with Eld. F. B. Rolfe, and had an excellent meeting. Here I succeeded in obtaining twenty members for the society. 26th.—Attended the funeral of James Applebee, in company with several ministers of other denominations. Preached at the Governor's Road on the 27th; also on New Year's Day. Got seventeen new members. Dec. 28th.—Preached at Northfield. Got ten members. Jan. 4th, 1854.— Preached near Port Credit; and on the 5th made my way to Whitby again, after an absence of about three weeks. Found all well. Visited some of the brethren in Whitby on the 6th and 7th. On the 8th, which was Sunday, was sick at home, in consequence of taking cold, and over-doing. Went to Orono on the 12th, to meet the Missionary Board. Had not a quorum, and could do no business. Went to Pickering on the 14th; obtained twelve members; preached on Sunday, the 15th; and on the 16th returned to Whitby. Spent Sunday, 22nd, in Newmarket, 29th in Oshawa, and Feb. 5th in Whitechurch. 12th spent with the church in Clark. Went to Gwillimsbury on the 16th, and spent eight days visiting East and North Gwillimsbury and King. At Oshawa on the 26th. March 6th at Scarboro'; found things low, but did a little, and promised to visit them again. 12th spent at Clark. On the 19th preached in Pickering, and assisted at the ordination of Br. J Churchill."

Thus the record goes on month after month; and those best acquainted with the distance between the places mentioned, will best understand the amount of labor performed.

In 1853 another paper, called the *Christian Offering*, was started at Oshawa, by Eld. J. R. Hoag. This was more successful, and published at less sacrifice than the *Luminary*, from the fact that instead of purchasing, or trying to run a separate press, it was published in connection with the secular paper of the village. However, this never paid its way, and though its subscription list increased slowly from its beginning to its end, in some six years it too was merged into the *Palladium*. Eld. Henry did not take this paper on his shoulders as he had the *Luminary*, but was, all the same, one of its best supporters; was always connected with it, and always doing something, directly or indirectly, for its benefit.

In 1856 Eld. Henry was appointed one of the trustees of Starkey Seminary. He had always taken a deep interest in that institution, and had educated two of his children there. He always enjoyed the meetings of the Board, was ever at his post, and ready, there as elsewhere, to do his part.

He began to feel, about this time, that he had long enough sustained the relation of pastor to the church in Oshawa, and desired them to release him from the responsibility. He had borne the burden a long time, and though he felt a little weary, and the labors of an over-busy life were beginning to tell on him, yet it is doubtful if from any motive of personal ease he would have asked for release. Though no one else thought so, he felt that some younger, better educated man might better fill the place. After much hesitancy on the part of the church, they finally concluded to release him, and in doing so presented him with a beautiful Bible, accompanied by the following address, which was read before a large congregation, and afterwards printed in the *Offering*. Eld. J. F. Wade was chosen to fill the place which Father Henry left, and was never willing to take again, though he continued to manifest the same interest in its prosperity which he ever had done.

ADDRESS

Presented by the Oshawa Christian Church to Eld. Henry, with a Bible, on his resigning the Pastoral charge:—

"Dear Elder and Brother,—We feel in duty bound to grant your request, and liberate you from the care and responsibility you have borne so long. But while we accede to your request, we do so regretfully.

"We feel it will be hard for another to occupy the place you have filled so well; yet we indulge the hope that in times of trial and perplexity you will still aid us by your counsel and your prayers. Many years ago, when we were few in number, encompassed in darkness and surrounded by enemies, we committed to your hands the trust which we receive back again to-day. Through all the varied events of our past career, in adversity and prosperity, we have looked to you, under Christ, our living Head, for advice and encouragement, and never have you betrayed the confidence reposed in you. When others have failed us, you have remained true to our interest; you have sympathized with us in our sorrows, and rejoiced in our rejoicing. Never, never can we forget your faithful admonitions, your self-sacrificing toils, your unremunerated labors in our behalf, and in the cause of our common Master.

"We feel that to you, under God, we owe our present prosperity; and that in your disinterested zeal we have enjoyed a blessing which falls to the lot of few churches. While the house in which we worship, and we who regularly assemble here are your witnesses, many others, who are scattered abroad over the world, can testify to your faithfulness; and some who have already passed through the swellings of Jordan, are seals of your ministry in this place. You are endeared to us by all the ties which a long and friendly association weave around the heart. We feel for you that affection which we must ever feel for one whom a long acquaintance has proved to be true-hearted, and who has borne with us the burden of many a conflict. But now that you wish to retire from this responsible post, that you may be more at liberty to travel and visit the churches, we yield to your desires; at the same time, we pray that we may be favored with another, who will be as faithful to our wants as you have been.

"In parting, we wish to bestow a small memento, to remind you of our love.

"Accept, then, this token of our gratitude. It is as a faint memorial of our affection, we present to you this transcript of God's love to man. In so doing, we feel that we have chosen the fittest token to express obligations such as ours, and the most becoming testimonial of labors such as yours, as both you and ourselves are pledged to it as our only rule of faith and practice. We well know it has long been the man of your counsel, a light to your path, and a lamp to your feet. We need not remind you that you may derive solace in your declining years, from the same promises from which you gathered strength for the conflict of active life.

"In conclusion, we would say, you may be assured our prayers and best wishes will follow you wherever you go. May your *last* days be emphatically your *best* days! May you see the churches, for whom you have labored so much, prosper, and live many years to bless them by your admonitions and prayers! May you enjoy the richest of earthly blessings, and the uninterrupted sunshine of God's love! May your death be peaceful and happy; and when Christ comes to make up His jewels, may you, who have so long sown the precious seed in tears, return with songs of rejoicing, and bring your sheaves with joy into the garner of our God!

"In behalf of the church,

"P. A. H.

"Oshawa, 1856."

Eld. Henry writes, under date of July, 1859:

"On the 26th June, I started from home, in company with my wife, whose health was poor, to attend the New York W. C. Conference, to be holden in Royalton, Niagara County, New York. We arrived there in the afternoon of the 27th, in time to hear a discourse from Eld. Davis, who is one of the pioneers who have borne the burden and heat of the day. He preached an excellent discourse, which moved the hearts of God's children. In the evening, Eld. Burlingame preached. Next morning we met in prayer and conference meeting, after which Eld. Weeks gave us a very feeling discourse. He was followed by our good brother Hoag, who formerly labored with us in the Province.

"At four o'clock the President, J. D. Childs, preached from the words, 'Come and see.' Eld. Childs is a strong man, a noble preacher, and an excellent chairman for Conference business. In conclusion, I will say, I was highly pleased with the Conference. It was a pleasure to shake hands with so many ministers of the gospel. Some of their heads are blossomed for the grave; but their hearts are animated by the love of God. To all those dear friends who were so kind to us, we tender our sincere thanks.

"T. Henry."

Less actively engaged in preaching than in earlier years, but not less interested in the advancement of the cause of Christ, he was always ready to assist others. For some years Eld. H. Burnham spent considerable time in each year in holding revival meetings in Canada. Father Henry devoted much of his time to assisting him in these efforts, and conveying him to the meetings. He also kept our denominational papers well informed as to the results of these meetings; and that impressible revivalist was in the habit of saying, he could preach better when he had Bro. Henry to say Amen.

Whatever ministers came from United States to Canada, they were sure to come to Father Henry's. His location favored their doing so; and then he was always ready with his own conveyance to take them from place to place, assisting at their meetings, and doing them, and those among whom he went, more good by his cheerfulness and cordial sympathy than half the sermons did. He was not troubled with that fearful disease, ministerial jealousy, but was always glad to see others have a good time.

Joy and Sorrow.

CHAPTER X.

CHRISTIAN OFFERING—HYMN-BOOK—JOY AND SORROW.

IN the autumn of 1859, Moses Cummings, then editor of the *Christian Palladium*, paid a visit to Canada, and Father Henry accompanied him on a trip through some of the churches. Cumings wrote as follows in the next issue of the *Palladium* :—

"*Thomas Henry.* This brother must excuse this allusion to him. He was the companion of our journey in the Province. His kindness will never be forgotten. We have placed his name alone, because like the sun he shines all over Christian Canada. His name, and his labors as a minister, are felt in every church. It was said of J. C. Calhoun, that he was not the *sun* of South Carolina, but *South Carolina* itself. This remark will give our readers an idea of the relation Bro. Henry sustains to the Christian cause in Canada."

The object of Mr. Cummings visit to Canada was to consummate the union of the *Christian Offering* with the *Palladium*. When it was done, Thomas Henry's name was placed as corresponding editor at the head of the columns devoted to Canada. For years previous to this, he had been one of its executive board.

Again in Oct. he writes: "I always love to hear and tell good news, and believe that to be one of the objects of a religious paper. On Saturday, 10th inst., I started by railway for Wellers Bay, a distance of 80 miles. We had a good meeting. After the sermon about forty spoke, and ten or twelve prayed; five spoke for the first time.

"The revival at Haldimand is a source of rejoicing. I should like to hear from Castleton, to know if the believers there have been baptized and organized into a church, on the foundation of the Apostles and Prophets.

"October, 1858, as it is well known, I was appointed by the Conference to attend the General Convention in N.Y. city, which has just closed, some of your readers may expect to hear something from me respecting it. I left home on the morning of the 5th inst., and proceeded by way of Toronto and Hamilton to Niagara, crossed Suspension Bridge, and went on by way of Rochester and Albany to N.Y. city. I found the Convention just organized at the Mercantile Library lecture room, and presented my letter which was duly received. To me it was truly gratifying to meet so many Christian ministers and some of other denominations, among whom was Dr. Bellows of N.Y. The hand of time has swept away many of our old ministers, and but few of the pioneers remain; yet we have nothing to fear, for their places are filled by an army of strong young men, who are able to hold the ground obtained by their fathers. I do not wish to anticipate the Minutes, and will only speak for myself. It was one of the pleasantest seasons I have ever enjoyed, and one that will be remembered by me until my dying day."

Thus, as we turn over the pages of past volumes of the *Offering* or *Palladium*, we find scattered all along such little choice letters or bits of Journal, which show not only his interest in the good cause, but his ability to gather up and communicate useful information, and interesting items of news. During these years, the Christians in the States were engaged in an earnest effort to pay for Antioch College. Though not particularly identified with this enterprise, Father

Henry was ready to help, as he always was, in every good work. He was their agent in Canada, and exerted himself to bring their claims before the people and to collect and remit what money he could to them.

Elder T. Garbutt published, for a few years, a monthly magazine at Castleton, Ont. In the number for Aug., 1866, we find the following:

"There is no name more endeared to the people called Christians, than that of Elder Thomas Henry. He has spent the greater part of his life in Canada—that life has been devoted to the cause of Christ. He was called on to stand forth in the defence of our views, at a period when those views met with strong opposition; but endowed with great grace, indomitable perseverance, a clear head and warm heart, he has fought a good fight, and adorned his profession; though now somewhat advanced in age, he is an able and acceptable preacher, *beloved and respected by all who know him.*"

I will introduce here an article written by Father Henry immediately after the General Convention of 1866. It was written for some of our periodicals and probably published, but I do not recollect.

"JOY AND SORROW."

"Solomon well understood human life when he said 'To every thing there is a season, and a time to every purpose under the heavens—a time to be born and a time to die ; a time to weep and a time to laugh ; a time to mourn and a time to dance.'

"This is the experience of all, and never have I felt more conscious of it than during the past month. My wife has been much afflicted with lameness. My son Albert, his wife and child have all had a run of typhoid fever, and to her it proved fatal. Albert and his child were first attacked with the fever, and when partially recovered, went with his wife to his brother George's home near Bowmanville, for a little change of air, rest and good nursing. Albert became worse for a time, and his wife was attacked with the same fever. This was just at the time of our Annual Conference, which met at Newmarket. Apprehending no serious consequences, and being very anxious to attend, I went to the Conference in company with the delegates from Oshawa, and Bro. Lawton of the N.Y. W. Conference. This was the forty-first session of our Conference, not one of which have I failed to attend. I was very unwell during the Conference, but preached once on Saturday ; after which we had an old fashioned fellowship meeting. It did my heart good to hear from the veterans, who espoused the cause over forty years ago in those never to be forgotten days, when we enjoyed the labors of such men as Morrison, Church, Blodget, Baily, McIntyre, Blackmar, and Goff. I was also much encouraged to see so many of the young who have enlisted to fight the fight of faith.

"On my return from Conference, I learned that my son was better, but his wife was very low. That week Bro. Simeon Swett and wife arrived at our place, on their way to attend the Convention, to be held in Marshall, Michigan. They stayed over Sunday, and Bro. Swett preached twice. During the morning service we got word that my daughter-in-law was dead. She had peacefully breathed her last, in hope of a glorious resurrection. On Monday we went down to Bowmanville, and brought back her lifeless remains, and deposited them in their last resting place in the burying-ground at Port Oshawa. How sad to see that blighted flower so early placed in the grave— only 23 years of age. Daughter, wife, mother, Christian—farewell!

"On the same evening, in company with my daughter-in-law, Mrs. P. A. Henry, I started for the Convention on the Grand Trunk Railway. The next morning we found ourselves entering the State of Michigan. At Port Huron we fell in company with Rev. J. W. Haley, Mrs. Cartwright and Mrs. Bennet from Somerset, Mass., and Mrs. Chase from Parma, all on their way to the Convention in Marshall, which place we reached about 11 p.m., and found two brethren waiting to conduct us to their comfortable homes.

"The Convention was one of the largest and best I

have ever attended; but I will leave reports to the reporters and editors present, and simply say, to me it was a joyful season and a foretaste of Heaven."

That was what Father Henry said about the Convention and the events preceding it. I remember them all. How worn and tired I was with nursing my sister-in-law; and yet how patient the dear young creature had been, and Albert too. He preaches now at Medway, N.Y., but did not look then as though he would ever preach; and the little girl—dear little Bertie is a fine, healthy girl now, and lives with her father in the little parsonage at Medway; but she was very sick then, and had to learn to walk the second time. It was a sad time. Father, mother, and little girl all in bed sick at once. The mother died, and father and child got better, and went up to Father Henry's, where the youngest, little Myrtle, had been all the time with her grandma. She lives with that grandmother yet, who is lame and feeble, and needs her; but she has no mother or grandfather now. It was one of those seasons we never forgot.

How kind and thoughtful it was in Father Henry to come and take me away to the Convention, and give me such a treat; how refreshing was the change from the sad, sick room, with all its disagreeable accompaniments. Even the motion of the cars, and the swift passage through the air were exhilarating—and how could I but enjoy the cool, bright October day, with its bracing atmosphere and showers of crimson and yellow leaves: it was a pleasant journey. Father Henry was kind and entertaining, as he always was when travelling. When we met those friends from the East, they seemed tired and dispirited, but father's pleasant, cheerful conversation made them lively again. I remember all about the Convention, too: it was the first I had attended. There were men there about whom I had heard and read since childhood; for my father was a Christian minister, too, and I had read the *Palladium* since I was a little girl. Long years had my father been dead, and his name is now nearly forgotten in the denomination, though there may be a few still living who remember Joshua Hayward, who was as truly a martyr to the cause of Christ as those who sealed their testimony at the stake.

It was nothing to me that I was an unnoticed stranger. I saw and heard the faces and voices which I had never seen and heard before; and yet they seemed familiar to me. We returned home and a great many of our Easterm friends and ministers came with us. We had a good visit, and a grand old meeting. How much brighter everything looked than when we went away?

JOY AND SORROW.

How rapidly oscillates the pendulum of existence between joy and sorrow? In life's moments of greatest fulness how near are we to death? Even then, the stealthy steps of the destroyer were among us, and we knew it not.

In a very few days after our return, Mrs. Eliza Guy, eldest daughter of Father Henry, was taken with the same fever. She was one of the most lovable and amiable of women, with a chastened sweetness of manner which attracted all who came near her. She was a wife. The mistress of a pleasant home, and the mother of five children. Our prayers, and the efforts of medical men, the sorrow of her husband, and the anguish and tears of her children, were alike unavailing. Just as the bleak December weather swept away the last vestiges of that summer brightness and beauty which she loved so well, she closed her weary eyes, and slept on Jesus' breast.

The following paper I contributed at the time to the "Ladies' Social" of Oshawa, of which she was a loved and active member.

"How mysterious is that change we call death—how silent and inexplicable its approach? Familiar forms stand by our side. They share with us the pleasures and sorrows, the needs and capabilities of our common existence: but disease makes its appearance, the head droops heavily on its pillow, and the familiar face grows thin and pale. We too have felt pain, and can sympathize with them. Care and sympathy are sweet, but unavailing. Let the intimacy between human hearts be ever so close, each is to all intents alone, and must struggle alone with that invisible power. A power superior to all our skill, stronger than the most potent will, seizes the helm and the little barque glides slowly out on the receding billow of death. Powerless as infants we watch them, feeling rather than seeing the distance widen between us, until they are gone—gone from us while yet in our midst! But why, it is asked, should we select such a gloomy subject for contemplation? One wiser than we are has said: 'It is better to go to the house of mourning, than the house of feasting.' Not alone, however, to the house of mourning will I lead those who accompany me in these thoughts.

"Death furnishes occasion for the highest triumphs of our spiritual nature. As the glory of the nocturnal heavens would never be seen, but for the dark shadow of the brooding wing of night. So human faith, love, and courage, have been revealed to us in a light in which nothing less terrible than death could present them.

"Death gives a deeper significance to life. Was there no such thing as death to be dared or endured, how soon would those pictures of heroism, which the human mind never tires of contemplating, vanish? And where would be the martyr's crown and song?

JOY AND SORROW.

If it is an awe-inspiring thing to see one in the quiet of the sick chamber, when disease has loosened the ties that bind to existence, yield without fear to its influence, how much more so to see one in the fulness of health and strength deliberately stake life on a principle, and meet death in the sternest form, rather than sacrifice the *truth?* Yet this is the history of martyrdom—the history of the thousands who have lain down their lives for Christ. A spark of the same Divinity, darkened indeed by ignorance and superstition, gleams forth in the Hindoo wife who immolates herself on the funeral pile of her husband.

" I have seen the aged saint in the Indian summer of his existence, waiting for the ice-king's approach; waiting in the land of Beulah, at the end of his pilgrimage, for the message to summon him across the river; and when the hour came, closing his eyes.

'" Like one who wraps the drapery of his couch,
Around him, and lies down to pleasant dreams."'

" I have seen a young girl in the first bloom of youth, when life wears the most enchanting aspect, and sunshine, song and flowers were around her, cheerfully close her eyes on earthly bliss, to open them on the unfading glories of eternity.

" Here we have seen Sister Guy, a mother—a tender mother,—whose whole soul went out in yearning affection for the little ones whom God had given her, leave them in this cold world, trusting in the promise of the faithful One, and die without a murmur. Were there no death, we should never know there were such sublime capabilities in the human soul!

"Do you say it is still to the house of mourning that my thoughts have led? It may be so; but the house of mourning here, has become the vestibule to the house of feasting on high—our Father's house, the mansion our Saviour has gone to prepare; where the marriage supper of the Lamb shall be spread. At that feast, the humble and lowly of earth, the faithful and loving ones, shall be honored guests. Thither has Sister Guy preceded us, and thither follow our hearts.

> "We miss thee sister, and must mourn
>   Sadly thy loss;
>   Our human hearts, with anguish torn,
>   Faint with the cross.
>
> "There seemed so much for thee to do;
>   Thy ready hand
>   So well its work and mission knew,
>   Thy feet to stand.
>
> "In duty's path, and walk, or run
>   With constant care;
>   Oh, was thy work so early done,
>   Our sister dear?
>
> "Our Father took what He had given,—
>   One loved so well,
>   With angels in the far-off heaven,
>   Henceforth to dwell.
>
> "But though removed, she liveth still,
>   In deed and thought,
>   And words of love. It is God's will:
>   'The good die not.'"

CHAPTER XI.

FULNESS OF YEARS—YORK PIONEERS.

FATHER Henry was now in the full enjoyment of a "green old age"; with health and vigor such as seldom fall to the lot of men of his years; with an easy competence in property, and a large and respectable family, settled comfortably around him. Ten sons and three daughters survive him; all but one son living within a day's travel of his home. His fourth son, E. E. Henry, lives in Leavenworth City, Kansas.

During these years, time, and the labors of an exceptionally busy life, began to tell on his strong frame; but he was active and energetic, and contested every inch of ground which age and disease won from him.

When the Biblical School enterprise was started, he at once became one of its firmest friends. He was chosen one of its trustees, and retained that position and his interest in the Institute until the day of his death. His last journey was made to attend a meeting of the Board of Trustees, of which he had never missed one.

In a "Pen Sketch of the Board of Trustees of the Christian Biblical Institute," which appeared in the *Herald* in 1870, we find the following:

"Thomas Henry, of Canada, is the oldest member of the Board, being now over seventy years of age, and has been preaching forty-two years. He is a native of Ireland, and is one of the youngest men of his age outside of the United States. He is yet young and buoyant in spirits, believes in improvement, and is not one of those old men who think wisdom and virtue will die with their generation. He is full six feet in height, well proportioned, sandy complexion, hair naturally light is becoming somewhat gray and thin on the head. He is thoroughly in sympathy with the Bible principles of the Christians, and wide awake to all our denominational enterprises. He is bitterly opposed to selfishness, and to sectional and rival interests in our denomination, but earnestly desires that the east, west, centre and Canada, be heartily united in our publishing interests and Biblical School. He is of a sociable and affable disposition, and a useful minister and highly esteemed citizen."

Though Father Henry was prudent and economical to the last degree in business affairs, yet he had a liberal hand, and an ear ever open to the calls of distressed humanity. There was withal a touch of chivalry in his character. He never saw a woman, high or low, in trouble without at least attempting to assist her. There never was a poor widow or washerwoman who knew him, who would not sooner apply to him for help than almost any other person. At one time, some years ago, father was travelling at night on one of our lake steamers bound West. A large number of German emigrants were in the steerage. Some time in the night one of these emigrant women was taken suddenly very ill. Her husband, unable to speak but few words in English, made an outcry, calling in his broken language for a doctor. If medical men heard they did not make themselves known. Aroused by the outcry, Father Henry came from his berth in the cabin, as there were no staterooms on the boat. He soon learned the state of affairs, and knew what to do, if no one else did. He went at once to the steward's room; by his peremptory manner induced that functionary to vacate his domain. Then descending to the steerage, took the woman in his arms, carried her to the room, deposited her in the berth, and then went where he knew a physician was lying, and as peremptorily requested him to go and attend to the patient.

Such incidents need no comment; they stamp the insignia of moral greatness on the man, in characters which all may read.

At one time the stream which flows past his place had so overflown its banks as to render it impossible for foot passengers to cross without being badly wetted, the water being a foot and a half deep over the road. Father Henry, at work near the road, saw a woman on the opposite side who seemed very anxious to get across. He took off boots and hose, rolled up his pants, and went and got the woman, brought her across in his arms, and set her dry shod on the shore. Yet so prudent was he in all his intercourse with the opposite sex, and so apparent was the disinterestedness of his intentions, that the breath of calumny never was thrown on him from that direction.

Few ministers preached more funeral sermons or solemnized more marriages than did Father Henry. His ready sympathy with both joy and sorrow made him an acceptable guest at the one, and a welcome friend and efficient comforter at the other; and he frequently travelled long distances for both purposes, and officiated among all classes.

A negro living not far from his home, and one who had been in his employ sometimes, had a wife and adopted daughter of the same color. Cupid being no respecter of colors at least, makes as sad havoc with dark hearts as light ones, and this negro's adopted daughter being taken in his noose, wished to slip her head into the noose matrimonial with a "gentleman" of her own color. Preparations were made for celebrating the affair in what they considered fine style. Elder Henry must perform the ceremony. When the ceremony was ended, the groom appeared a little bashful, and the company slightly at loss to know what was to be done next. Father Henry, ever willing to help such as need help, suggested that the groom should salute his bride. The groom was about to comply, when the old darkey interfered : " No, no: the Dominie must have the first kiss." The Dominie probably felt a slight shudder at this result of his efforts to please, but as he was not in the habit of shirking in a hard spat, he stepped forward, and impressed on the lips of the blushing (?) bride a kiss, which was, no doubt, more gratifying to her than agreeable to him ; and will probably be handed down by tradition in the family, with as much pride as the little French girl's kiss from General Grant.

Father Henry was very fond of children, and his grandchildren will carry to their graves pleasant memories of " Grandpa's parties." These parties were given on the 24th of May, and the grandchildren were all invited. The children also were welcome if they came, but the grandchildren were the honored guests. We shall always remember the long table, surrounded by children, with grandpa at the head dispensing the good cheer provided for the occasion, with a face scarcely less bright and happy than the children around him.

In 1871, Father Henry wrote to the *Herald:* "I have finished my winter's campaign of over thirteen hundred miles travel, partly by my own and partly by public conveyance. On the 5th of February I was visiting a dear sister residing in Jeddo, Michigan. In the forenoon of that day I preached there; and in the evening, by Elder H. Hayward's request, I spoke to his congregation near Farewell's Mills. At both of these meetings were present a large number of persons formerly from Canada; several of whom I had baptized. Elder Hayward's labors in this place have been blessed. A number have confessed the Saviour, and intend to go forward in baptism soon. From here I went to Romeo, to attend the Michigan State Convention, and the dedication of the beautiful chapel erected by the dear friends in that place. Here I had the privilege of visiting Elder Deering, and a number of the good brethren and sisters and their families. On Monday morning I bade farewell to my brethren in Romeo, expecting to meet them no more until we reach the promised land. From here Elder D. W. Moore accompanied me to the Grand Trunk Railway Station, at Ridgeway, where we parted, Brother Moore going West, and I East. I reached home on the 14th, and found that Elder Childs, of the State of New York, had been at Oshawa, and preached two or three sermons to good acceptance, and gone to Orono in company with Elder Fowler, to hold a general meeting there. I made my way to Orono, where I had the pleasure of listening to two sermons from him, which will not soon be forgotten. On the 21st I parted with this good brother and faithful minister of the cross, at the Oshawa station.

"On the 24th I went to Brougham, and visited some friends there, and next day reached Bloomington in time for their fellowship meeting. Here I found Elder Tatton engaged in a good work. He has lately baptized 28, and received 30 into church fellowship. The next day I preached for him in that place, and in the evening at Ringwood. Some interest is awakened in that place too. Four have made a start for heaven. Elder Tatton is working too hard; I hope the churches will not be forgetful of him. On the third of March I started in company with my son John, and reached his pleasant home the same evening. The next day I was conveyed by my grandson, a distance of fifteen miles, to Drayton, in good time for their fellowship meeting. Here I met my brother, Elder William Henry, who has charge of that district. We had a good time. The next day I preached to a full house. On Monday the 6th, my brother William took me to Minto; here I remained three days visiting friends and resting. During this time I wrote my will, thinking that perhaps I was as free from care as I should ever be. While doing this solemn work, my mind was not only on the work, but on the promised land. If this should be my last work, I hope I may be able to say as did Paul when about to combat the last enemy : ' I am now ready to be offered, and the time of my departure is at hand. I have fought the good fight, I have finished my course, I have kept the faith,' " etc.

Father Henry's attachments were strong and enduring. He never forgot the friends of his early years. He loved his ministering brethren, particulary those who had borne the " burden and heat of the day " with him, with an undying affection. His sympathy and attachment for the denomination with which he was connected never diminished ; but one denomination did not hold all his friends. He found congenial spirits among all. Prominent among these were three men with whom he had been intimate for years, and for whom his friendship seemed to increase as the years passed, and he felt they were nearing that time when the shadow of death would dim the light of those pleasant hours he spent in their companionship. These men were J. B. Warren, Esq., one of the oldest residents of Oshawa, and one of its most esteemed citizens. Another was Senator John Simpson, well known to the inhabitants of Ontario, and Captain John Trull, of Bowmanville. These four often met each other and spent a few hours in social converse. The first to leave the ranks was Mr. Warren, who died some months before Father Henry. When informed of his death father said: "John is gone, it will be my turn next." His words were verified. The other two yet remain.

In 1875 the Canadian Government settled a pension on the few surviving soldiers of the war of 1812, and Father Henry was among the number who received it. The amount was small, yet highly prized by him, and no doubt by others, as a memento of past years and stirring scenes.

The same year he formed a connection with a society called the "York Pioneers," which was composed of the few still left of the soldiers who were in York or its vicinity during those same troublous times. These old men met once a year in Toronto and partook of a dinner together, which was enlivened by speeches, songs, toasts, and anecdotes of olden times, and particulary of their soldier life; and thus they keep alive the memories and friendships of the past. The following extract from a letter refers to one of these gatherings:—"I should have answered your letter before had I been at home when it arrived. Having been invited by Mr. R. H. Oates, chairman of the standing committee of the York Pioneers to partake of a dinner at the Walker House on the 14th instant, I was there when your letter came. We had indeed a very pleasant time, meeting and greeting so many of the veterans, and shaking with them the friendly hand. Nearly all my friends and acquaintances of the times of 1812 have gone to the narrow house appointed to all living. I enquired for John Bright, and found him in the company, in his 83rd year. I had not met him since we served together in the York Militia, where he received a slight wound."

After Father Henry's death the following letter was received by the family : " To the family and friends of our late respected Brother, Thomas Henry, member of the York Pioneers. At the regular monthly meeting of the Society to-day, it was moved and adopted, that the heartfelt sympathies and condolence of the members be communicated to the friends and relatives of our late highly esteemed Brother, which I hereby have pleasure in conveying to you in all love, remaining most respectfully and affectionately yours,

"ALEXANDER HAMILTON,
"Secretary, York Pioneers."

CHAPTER XII.

THE CLOSING SCENE.

DISEASE, with the commencement of 1878, took hold of our father in a form which even his strong will and great energy were powerless to resist. For two whole months he, who had never before succumbed to disease for a single week in his life, was confined to the house. His sufferings were severe, and the confinement itself was a heavy trial to one of his active habits. But he would not be debarred from meeting his friends who came from far and near to see him; and not a day passed but visitors were in his room. He said repeatedly that their society did him good, and he should recover sooner or live longer than if kept in solitude. The kindnesses which he received during his sickness from his own family, as well as the immediate circle of friends around him, and the interest manifested by all in his recovery, touched his heart deeply; and the first use he made of his convalescence was to write letters overflowing with gratitude to God, and love to his friends for all the mercies, and all the kindly deeds, of which he had been the recipient during the dark hours of suffering.

The skilful treatment of Dr. W. S. Clark, Clairvoyant Physician, 171 Jarvis Street, Toronto, and the care of his friends, under the blessing of a kind Providence, wrought a change for the better, and when March with its wide-spread, sunny wings wafted in the glorious springtime, we knew that he was better, and felt that he was to be with us yet a time longer. When the warm April days came he rode out in his carriage, and began to feel that he might be able to attend the trustee meeting at the Biblical School. He did not feel well enough to go alone, and by his request I went with him. There are pleasant memories connected with this journey, which will live while life lasts. We crossed the Lake on the 6th of May, and stayed the first night at the residence of that gifted and accomplished Christian lady, Miss Cairns, M. D., of Rochester. On the way from there to Stanfordville, we fell in company with Rev. D. W. Moore and Deacon Chase, who were also on their way to the meeting. How much he enjoyed their society—he seemed almost well and young again. How cordially he was welcomed everywhere, and with what tenderness and reverence he was treated by Dr. Craig and his amiable family, and the other members of the Board. No one was better pleased to see him in his place, or more thoughtful of his comfort than Hon. D. Clark, who has done so much for that School. Before we left this place he ·presented father with a gold watch, as a token of the high esteem in which he was held. We spent two pleasant days at Dr. Craig's residence—*more than pleasant* they were to me, for Sister Craig, that sweet woman who has since gone to be with the Saviour, was a playmate of mine when we were little girls, and together we went to school in the little brown school-house on the shore of Schuyler's Lake. We had not met for more than twenty-five years, and it was a dear re-union.

From Stanfordville we made a little trip to New York City on a Hudson River boat, and enjoyed a glimpse of the far-famed scenery of the river's banks. Spent a day in New York, and as everybody else does who goes there, rode on the elevated railroad, and visited Central Park, &c. J. C. Brush, whose name is familiar to the readers of the *Herald*, was very kind to us, and father enjoyed the sight-seeing as much as I did. He was very feeble when we left home, but had gained in strength and spirits every hour. On our way home, we called and spent four days with my brother, Rev. A. Hayward, of West Lawrence, and one at the residence of Rev. C. E. Peake, in St. Johnsville.

After returning from this trip, father kept quite comfortable during the summer, made several tours among the churches, and in September attended the General Convention held in Franklin, Ohio.

Through the next winter he was feeble again, but not so ill as he had been the previous winter. In the spring he did not recuperate as much as we hoped he would, but still he attended the Biblical School meeting once more. This time Mother Henry accompanied him, and they stopped on the way to visit their son, A. N. Henry, who was preaching at Medway, Green Co., New York. On their return they attended the New York C. Conference, held at Rural Grove, where their son was ordained to the work of the ministry. It was a solemnly joyful occasion to his parents. May the mantle of our departed father fall on this son who is rising up to fill the vacancy he has left in the ranks of Zion!

Through this summer father kept rather feeble, and we feared he would not survive another winter, but we were not prepared for what came.

On the evening of Sunday, Sept. 14th, he was taken very ill. It was a night of fearful suffering for father, and mother was so lame she could not walk a step. Fortunately his only surviving brother, Elder Wm. Henry was with him, to support and comfort him through this night of agony. The next day he seemed better, and on Tuesday morning his brother went to Orono, to attend the Conference, which he had hoped to attend with his only brother—only these two left of the family. I went to see father on Wednesday. He was very sick; still we did not think his end so near. On Friday the word came he was much worse. Oh, how long it seemed to take, to get the horse and buggy ready and go to him! What a sad change! Many of the family were already with him. His eldest surviving daughter, Mrs. Lizzie Dearborn, with loving tenderness had taken her mother's place, at her father's side; I joined her, and we left him no more until that watcher came, from whose presence the living turn away. Telegrams were sent for the absent sons, and for his brother, and D. W. Moore, who were at Orono. They came in the afternoon, he knew and conversed with them. George, my husband, was at Montreal, and did not arrive until Saturday morning; he knew him, but was only able to speak in broken sentences. From this time he sank rapidly away. Throughout his sickness—through those six fearful days, he had suffered intensely; but oh, how patient, how affectionate, how grateful! When the work of life, which calls out the sterner qualities of the man was done, the gentler virtues of the heart shone with increased lustre. When faith and hope waited but a little time for their fulfilment, holy love eternal in its office, spread its brooding wings over all. How often he had kissed us as we bent over him, or asked us to kiss him! How many times he had told us he loved us, and asked for his dear companion to be drawn in her chair to his bedside, that he might kiss her, and ask if he had been kind to her. All this was done now. His eyes would follow the loved forms around his bed, but he would speak our names no more upon earth—nevermore! nevermore! *He was not, for God had taken him!*

Elder D. W. Moore, who, by his request, preached

his funeral sermon, has given the following account of the funeral, which is much better than any of us could have done; also of his last interview with him. *We* saw as in a dream what was passing around us, *we* only fully realized that *father was dead*, they were going to bury him out of our sight; or we looked and listened if perchance we might hear the rustle of spirit wings, or catch the gleam of the white robe which is the "righteousness of the saints."

Mr. Moore says: "He sent for me to come and see him from Orono. I came into the sick room about three o'clock, Friday afternoon. He recognized me at once, and exclaimed, 'Oh, my dear Brother Moore, here you are! I am glad to see you. Kiss me!' Then he asked me to preach his funeral sermon, and give his love to the brethren in the States. We bowed around his dying bed, had a season of prayer, and bade this good brother a final farewell on earth. After this he gradually sank away until the next afternoon, when he quietly breathed his last.

"His funeral was attended at his residence on Tuesday, Sept. 23rd, at ten o'clock a.m. The service was conducted as follows: Scripture lesson by Rev. W. W. De Geer. Prayer by Rev. J. H. Shoults. Hymn by Rev. Wm. Percy. Sermon by Rev. D. W. Moore. Prayer by the same. Remarks by Rev. Mr. Clark, Methodist, of Oshawa. The remains were followed to their last resting place by 85 carriages, and there were eighteen ministers at his funeral."

Once more the green turf on the little hill by the lake shore was broken, and Rev. Thomas Henry was buried there, not more than half a mile from his home. Sept. 23rd, 1879.

ABSTRACT

Of the discourse preached by Rev. D. W. Moore, at the funeral of Elder Thomas Henry, of Port Oshawa, Canada, September 23, 1879.

"For more than a century a huge and stately elm tree has stood out boldly and alone on an island just outside of the harbor at Kingston. During all these long years it raised its towering branches heavenward, while its strong roots, like sinews, struck deep and reached far down, laying hold upon the soil and entwining themselves around the rocks. Thus it stood amidst storm and sunshine, wintry blasts and summer breezes, like a pillar-cloud by day and by night to the mariners on the waters of Ontario for these hundred years.

"But the terrible gale which blew on lake and land last Wednesday morning tore this old landmark from its position and laid it, broken and prostrate, on the very soil from which it had drawn its strength and life. The roots which once had been strong as sinews were weakened by age. The boughs which were once young and elastic, and withstood many a storm, were broken. The grand old tree fell, to the sorrow and great regret of both citizen and sailor.

"So there has stood in this vicinity for more than half a century a noble man, who, in many respects, rose head and shoulders above those around him; a man who has stood the storms of adversity and persecution and the hardships of a pioneer life; a man who has been like a beacon-light along this lake shore for fifty years. But last Saturday afternoon the dark angel of the grave came and struck the fatal blow; the once strong man fell prostrate before the king of terrors, and Elder Thomas Henry was dead.

"On the very account of the exposed position in which it stood—because it was subject to winds and storms—that majestic old tree struck its roots deeper and firmer, and every limb and bough was strengthened by the conflict with nature. So with this noble man who has fallen. The very trials, exposures, and hardships through which he has passed made him strong in body, mind, and heart. But 'strong men shall bow themselves, and the life of man on earth shall fail.' * * * The messenger of death has by one blow struck down an affectionate husband, a loving father, a kind brother, a worthy citizen, a good neighbor, a consistent Christian, a faithful minister; and that good man whom we all learned to love and revere is no more on earth.

"Twenty-four hours before his departure, when, by his request, I was called to the bedside of my dear aged friend and brother, and saw him already entering upon the death-struggle, the words of David, as recorded in the first verse of the twelfth Psalm, came forcibly to my mind: 'Help, Lord, for the godly man ceaseth, and the faithful fail from among the children of men.' And after his expressed wish that I should preach his funeral sermon, I could think of no other words more appropriate for the occasion, or that better expressed the feelings of my heart.

"David, when he saw those who had been faithful and true, those who had been in the front of the battle and the thickest of the fight, those who had been good and firm—when he saw them falling and lost to the cause, his heart was filled with anguish; and feeling that the arm of man was too feeble, he cried out in the deep emotions of his soul, 'Help, Lord, for the godly man ceaseth, and the faithful fail from among the children of men.' When recalling how destitute was human comfort, he craveth help from God. So with me—so with us all. Observe how these two characteristics are here put together—the 'godly' and the 'faithful.' Let us briefly notice these two grand elements which go to make up the character of the best men of earth. * * Such are the men on whom God builds the world and the church; such are the men who are a blessing to mankind; such are the men with whom we love to meet, but loath to leave us; such men are the backbone and heart of society; they are the salt of the earth. * *

"As we have been speaking of the characteristics of the 'godly man and the faithful' have not your minds been naturally and inevitably turned to the dear good man whose obsequies we observe to-day? Do you not instinctively and without hesitation say that these traits of character, these deeds of duty and love, all belong to him? Will not this lone widow say, 'He was a good husband, faithful and true?' Do not these sons and daughters rise up and say, 'If ever children had a good father, we had?' These neighbors and acquaintances, all who hear me this day and all who knew him, will bear me witness, willing and heart-felt testimony, that whether in the pulpit, social circle, or in the family, he whose funeral rites we now attend was, in the full and complete sense of the term, a good man.

"But godly men cease, good men die, the faithful ones pass away. With them so much goodness goes out of the world. They have been a blessing to the world. We feel that we can ill-spare them. Hence their departure is a great loss, and when a good man dies we may well exclaim, 'Help, Lord, for the godly man ceaseth, and the faithful fail from among the children of men. * *

"In the removal of Father Henry the entire community has sustained an irreparable loss. The subdued tone in which the news of his death was communicated from lip to lip; the tears that flowed when the telegram was read before the Conference; the all pervading sadness it occasioned; the feeling manifested whenever his name was mentioned either in public or private; the heavy badges of mourning with which the church was draped on Sunday morning; the large and solemn assembly here this day—all these things attest in language stronger than words how deeply enshrined in the popular heart is the memory of him whose long and useful life has just closed.

"Elder Henry was blessed naturally not only with a fine, robust physical constitution, but also with an amiable, frank disposition, as well as good intellectual powers. Hence he was one of those men who leave a mark on the society in which they lived and a vacancy in the place they leave. He was one of those men who looked on the bright side of things and of life, and therefore was always of a cheerful disposition, scattering sunshine wherever he went.

"He was a man of industrious habits, a strict economist of time, always ready to do his duty, prompt to meet engagements and fulfil his promises, and strictly honest in all of his dealings. He was naturally of a devout disposition, always ready to show due reverence and respect to proper authority, to the house and worship of God; in fact, reverence was a special characteristic of him.

"Bro. Henry was a diligent student of the Bible. To him it was THE BOOK. He loved it, he studied it, he delighted to drink from the perennial springs of ever-fresh and ever-living truths of God's holy word. As the laborer relishes his meal and renews his strength by the bread he eats, so our departed brother was fed from the truths and doctrines of the Bible and made to rejoice in the promises of God.

"He was a man of uniform stability of mind. He was not changeable and fickle, still was reasonable and open to conviction, and when convinced was manly, noble enough to yield former opinions. He was firm in his belief, attached to his views, and yet not a bigot.

"As a consistent, straightforward man, he was a shining example to younger preachers who may follow him. Settled principles of conscious duty squared his character, his preaching, and his whole life.

"He was pre-eminently a man of peace, of expansive charity and large sympathy. He always looked on the charitable side of those who might have erred, and in having to deal with such, instead of being harsh, would always say it were better to err on the side of charity than severity. He was truly a friend to all, an enemy to none. To sum this point up in a word, he has been a man of the most forgiving, charitable Christian character.

"Elder Henry was a man who greatly delighted in Christian fellowship and communion. The house of worship, the fellowship meeting, the annual conferences, the general meetings of the brethren were like lovefeasts to his soul. He always commended love and good-will among Christians, and loved the good in all denominations. While he was firm and conscientious in his own religious views, and had a peculiar love for his Christian brethren, he was not narrow or sectarian. He enjoyed the esteem, rejoiced in the association and fellowship of the children of God anywhere. He was beloved and honored by the young people and children of his acquaintance, for whom he always had a cheerful word, and to whom he always gave wise and prudent counsel. Though he grew old in body, he never seemed to grow old in heart and spirit. He was of a meek and humble disposition, not rating himself above others, or stalking through the world with a high head and stiff neck thinking that everybody should pay great deference to him. He always appreciated a kindness, was really at heart thankful for any favor, hence made every one his friend. He felt under obligation for any and every act of kindness bestowed upon him, and was ever ready not only to acknowledge the favor, but to return the compliment by some kind deed.

"How many times during the two days since his death have we heard this remark, 'He will be missed.' Yes, he will be missed; first and most by her who has walked by his side and mingled with his joys and sorrows as his dearest earthly friend for fifty years.

"Missed by these sons and daughters who have so long had his noble example and Christian counsel.

"Missed by the old pioneers who may be still left to mourn their loss.

"Missed by the neighbors who have lived around

him, and associated with him in all the busy concerns of life.

"Missed by the very large circle of friends and acquaintances in all this section of the country.

"Missed by the church in Oshawa, of which he has been such a faithful member, minister, and supporter.

"Missed by the Canada Christian Conference, as all will testify who attended the session last week. The vacant chair sat by the pulpit at the very time that friends stood around his dying bed.

"Missed by the brethren on the other side of the lake, who so much enjoyed his visits. His house has always been the home of the Christian ministers from the States when visiting Canada. Many a brother from the other side has taken sweet counsel with him, and enjoyed the hospitalities of his home.

"Missed by the Board of Trustees of the Christian Biblical Institute. He was one of the three of us who have attended every annual meeting of the Board since its organization. It was there that the intimate love and friendship sprung up and grew and strengthened between us that has caused me to be your speaker on this sad occasion. I feel like a mourner with you to-day.

"Missed by the hundreds of readers of our religious paper, the HERALD OF GOSPEL LIBERTY, through whose columns he so frequently spoke to the brotherhood. He was our only regular correspondent from Canada.

"Missed he will be on earth, but greeted in heaven. Farewell, dear Bro. Henry, a short farewell; soon we shall mingle together again where gloom will be exchanged for glory and parting will be no more.

"He is at rest. The silver cord is loosed, the wheel broken at the cistern; the heart can beat no more, the light has faded out of the eye, the blood has ceased to flow, the last breath flies from the quivering lips, the soul leaves the tenement of clay, and the manly form lies down to sleep in death. The head is no more an aching head; those eyes shall no more be wet with tears; that heart shall no more weep with anguish, throb with grief, or be weighed down with sorrow; those limbs shall no more be racked with pain. He is at his journey's end, quiet and safe in the harbor of eternal rest—out of the reach of all storms, difficulties, and trials.

"Dear friends, do not mourn as those who have no hope. We cannot, would not say, 'Do not weep.' When you reflect on the virtues of the departed and the blessed associations you have had with him, your hearts are almost broken with tender feelings of affection and grief. At the tearing asunder of those sacred ties, well may we expect and allow some parting pangs and tears of sorrow. But look up through your sorrow and tears and heartachings and bereavement, and remember that your loss is his gain. Though he has ceased to move and talk and live amongst us, still 'he being dead yet speaketh.' He 'ceaseth,' but not entirely. He still lives in our hearts, in our memory, and speaks to us in his influence. Though he may rest from his labors, yet his works do follow him. Death may take away his earthly tabernacle from our midst, we may be compelled to bury his noble form from out of our sight, but it cannot hide from us that virtue we love, nor our blessed remembrance and admiration of the dear departed. So it is a wise and beautiful ministration by which the virtues, example, and memories of the dead speak to us, help us, comfort and bless us. If there were nothing more of our friends than the few fleeting years which they spend upon the theatre of this world, then, like Rachel, we might refuse to be comforted, because they are not. But, though gone, they are not forever lost. They live in light and glory. May the God of all grace comfort you and keep you and save us all in heaven at last.

(*Written for the Herald of Gospel Liberty.*)

DEATH OF ELDER THOMAS HENRY.

" Editorially—as also in an article from Elder D. W. Moore—the *Herald of Gospel Liberty* of October 4th bore to its readers a sorrowful message. It was an announcement of the death of that venerable and saintly man, Eld. Thomas Henry, of Oshawa, Canada. But few ministers in the denomination ever became better known or more widely beloved than Elder Henry. True, his face had not been seen nor his voice heard among the churches in general, but in the *Herald* all of us have often and for many years met this good man heart to heart, if not face to face. Precious the paper that introduces so many good men to our homes and breathes their Christly spirit into our households. But few men can give a glow of brotherly affection to their letters and newspaper articles as could Father Henry. Nor was this fire the forced kindling of dying coals. It was the glow of altar-flames that burned with an ever-increasing fervor. No letter, paragraph for paper, notice of meetings, or other form of written communication, lacked some sign of the soul-warmth peculiar to the writer. 'I must never write in a public or private way without saying something for Jesus, and something to strengthen and encourage my brethren,' seemed with him an ever-present and an ever-inspiring sentiment. In all the years of my editorship I found this one of the brightest jewel qualities of a man whose soul was as the setting of many priceless gems. How many knew of his numerous right-hand kindness kept in secrecy from the left, we know not. But through one of the *Herald* editors he often responded to calls for aid. Beautiful and sweetly-touching were some of the responses thus inspired in the hearts that read the hand of God in such timely help. A letter from a certain minister's widow was a wondrous breathing of that sweet pathos that kindled in Hagar's heart when for the sake of his thirsty and despairing handmaiden God came down from the heaven of ever-living fountains and opened a spring in the wilderness.

"Father Henry never made inquiry of the Lord whether he had not given enough or done his share.

Nay; but, as indicated in the sketch given by Brother Moore, he kept the armor on till laid off for the burial robe. His hand was active in service till just before his summons to reward.

"As a worker in the interest of denominational literature, the *Herald* never had a more active, constant, and steadfast friend than it had in Father Henry. No personal references ever prevented his co-operation in religious work. His loving, unselfish soul rose above all that was local and personal. It allied itself with all that was 'honest,' 'just,' 'pure,' 'lovely,' and of 'good report.' If any Christian of my acquaintance really loved all his brethren, ministry and laity, and all people of all theological persuasions, that man was Brother Henry. He possessed that rare and beautiful grace of being truly devoted to his own people in a truly non-sectarian spirit and example. Some persons are so sectarian in their professed *non*-sectarianism, as to be like one who rebukes anger in the spirit of a greater madness. But this minister of Christ vindicated the liberty of the gospel with consistency, discrimination, and ability. While his soul abhorred every thing that bordered on bigotry, his preaching allowed no laxity in relation to gospel essentials. His mind— or rather his heart—made not the mistake of those lax religionists in England, Germany, and now in America, who reject *theology* while avowing *Christianity*. Such rejection is a new stratagem of the enemy, and is meant for a stealthy undermining of 'the faith once delivered to the saints.' The systematic study of the Bible, in logical light and devout spirit, evolves from it the science of God and of divine things as set forth in the mediatorial scheme. Elder Henry, however, was not a menial to any ecclesiasticism of system or interpretation. He sought to draw his theology directly from the Bible, and to preach in such Bible language as avoided, as far as possible, the technical phraseology of the Schools. From the Bible he drew all his subjects, and grounded his sermons on the plain import of God's word. The simple power of scripture truth he wielded with great effect. He had no confidence in mere metaphysical and philosophical preaching. His sense of duty to perishing souls would not allow him to bring the gospel down to a level with perverted tastes, and philosophy, and science, falsely so called. He believed it the sole business of the pulpit to unfold, vindicate, and apply the truth of God's word. Souls could not live unconcerned nor churches remain inactive and lifeless under a ministry of such gospel simplicity and spiritual power. Through him Christ spake to the people in every discourse. He was not of that class of preachers described in Cowper's couplet:

> 'How oft when Paul has served us with a text,
> Has Epictetus, Plato, or Tully preached.'

"In a strictly literary sense, Father Henry was not a learned man. His sermons bore but little impress of human aids. They were coins of no human re-casting. They were bright and new from the mintage of mental fervor and soul-affection. His sermons were therefore fresh, original, and eminently spiritual. Too many sermons evince more reading than reflection, more food than digestion, more memory than comprehension. But Elder Henry had read much, had mastered much, and was indeed, quite familiar with the popular systems and current thought of the theological world. In addition to his reading he possessed a store or experience and observation from which he largely enriched his sermons and his conversation. Though destitute of large educational advantages in his early ministry, he would have no young minister at this day labor in a like embarrassment. Hence his great interest in the Biblical school, his appreciation of Brother Clark's benevolence, and his earnest desire that our people should further contribute to the pecuniary wants of the school and help young men to the great advantages there made so easily and economically available.

"In style, Father Henry displayed no polished eloquence. Plain, conversational, animated, loving, and often pathetic in speech, his words fell not short of the heart. What he lacked in rhetorical polish he supplied in spiritual power. All his face, nay, all his frame seemed to preach when fully under the inspiration of his theme. Words of inexpressible sweetness—words of tenderness—words of winning love would often pour forth from his soul. He could warn the sinner from Sinai, and from Olivet weep over souls from whom the heavenly good was hidden. Though his sermons were not after the strictest system—not always logically arranged—yet, judged by the higher rules of homiletics, they were enriched by qualities of the truest merit.

Hence the success of his ministry—but thank God for even the greater success of his Christian life.

'His preaching much, but more his practice wrought,—
A living sermon of the truths he taught.'

"In his family, among his neighbors, in the churches, in the conference session, on committees, acting as a trustee in important interests—in all things—everywhere, Father Henry was a man of peace, a man of kind words, a man of safe counsel. His feelings for all his family was that of pure, undying affection. In a lengthy conversation with him at the Oshawa quadrennial, as also in his many friendship letters, I could discover in what undying affection he held his companion and his children. The Lord sustain them in their loss and their grief!

"His affection for friends—for all his brethren—how ardent, how undying! When I was parting with him last June, at Stanfordville, New York—after that last session of the trustees in which he was ever to sit —after that last morning devotion with a family from whose embrace a loving soul was soon to ascend to glory in all the sanctified affection of wife and mother —with an earnest parting grip, Father Henry said : 'Farewell, Bro. Rush. It is not likely we shall ever meet on earth again. Give my love to my dear brethren in the States. Tell the friends at Franklin that I have not forgotten them. And the family that so kindly entertained me, (the sisters Maxwell) remember me sincerely to them. Now farewell, farewell; may we meet in heaven."

"As a member of the Board of Biblical school trustees I should like to say something of the valuable qualifications of Elder Henry, but my limits will not allow. The book of his biography will doubtless dwell upon the many interesting phases of the character of one who, as a husband, a father, a neighbor, a preacher, a pastor, a friend, and a counsellor was true to his lifework and triumphant in his death.

"H. Y. Rush.

"Franklin, Ohio."

IN MEMORIAM OF ELDER THOS. HENRY.

Sleep, faithful servant, friend of God,
  Thine hour of rest hath come at length;
Yes, sweetly sleep beneath the sod,
  Then wake to find immortal strength.

How grand the purpose of thy life!
  How grandly well thy work was done!
A foeman free from carnal strife,
  Thou'st fought the fight, the vict'ry won.

Oh! may thy heav'nly mantle fall
  Upon some youthful prophet fair,
Who, answering to the Master's call,
  Will strive as well to "do and dare."

And now, farewell, brave teacher, friend,
  No more we'll greet thy loving face,
Till we, like thee, have reached life's end,
  And found thee in eternal space.

D. E. Millard.

Honeoye Falls, N.Y., Oct. 3, 1879.

THE OLD HOME.

Not long since I went to visit Mother Henry, in the old home at Port Oshawa, where she lives with William, our youngest brother, and his amiable wife. Mother and Willie were both absent; but Eliza kindly welcomed me, and invited me to occupy mother's room—that room which she and father had so long occupied together; that room in which he had lain through days of suffering, and nights of anguish, and from which he went forth to return no more. I felt no superstitious dread of the place, but a solemn sense of the presence of something better than myself—something higher, nearer allied to the divine, than the ordinary surroundings of life.

Are the spirits of the departed ever permitted to come near to us? If so, Father Henry's spirit was near me that night. I seemed to see his face, to hear his voice. Memory also brought back forms and faces familiar, in the buried, but not forgotten, past— a throng of loved ones, who used to frequent the *Old Home* with me. I seemed to see them around me, to almost feel the touch of their hands.

The following imperfect lines are a faint sketch of the visions which floated before the eyes of my mind during

THE NIGHT IN THE OLD HOME.

Oh, the scenes of long ago
Float in shadows to and fro;
And the darkness of the night,
In their presence groweth light.
Gentle voices, loving words,
Like the distant song of birds,

Falling from a wondrous height,
Coming from above the night,
Drop upon my listening ear,
With a sound I love to hear.

Forms that here were wont to meet us,
Smiles that now no longer greet us—
Cherished visions—slowly pass,
Like reflections in a glass—
Gliding, melting into air.
Tiny children, soft and fair;
Sturdy boys with laughing faces;
Little girls with gentler graces;
Lovely maids with smile and song;
Young men, noble, brave, and strong;
Charming brides, and bridegrooms gay;
Loving mothers, thoughtful men;
Night of sorrow, festal day—
All are coming back again.

But among the well-known throng,
None seemed so bright, stay'd so long,
As the dear, benignant face,
That with patriarchal grace
Smiled upon the home-like scene;
Welcoming, with cordial mien,
All the loved ones gathered here.
Father, art thou not still near?
Where are all the loved ones gone?
Am I sitting here alone?
Ah, the loved ones! how they stray?
From the old homestead away!
Up and down the steeps of life,
Storm and sunshine, love and strife,
Are theirs. But the sleepers hid,
'Neath the coffin's folded lid,
Have rest—peace. Have they not more ?
No blessedness unknown before ?

E'en now I hear, in echoes sweet,
Faint whispers from the far-off sea,
Of boundless love and harmony,
That laves the silver-sanded shore,
Where those who walk shall sleep no more
The sleep of death. Are they not there?
Prophetic whispers answers, "*There!*"
Where those who love, their loved ones meet.

EXTRACTS FROM WRITINGS.

The following extract is from a sermon delivered by Elder Henry, I think before a Ministerial Association or something of that sort. I give it, not because it is better than many of his sermons, but because it is perhaps, a fair specimen of his style; and because I have it at hand, and few of his sermons were written. The others are short articles written for the *Christian Magazine*.

"The Bible is called by the Prophet Isaiah:.'The Book of the Lord'—by one of the ancients: 'The History of God.' It abounds in the most sublime descriptions of God's nature and perfections; from it we learn that He is a Spirit, infinite and eternal; unchangable in His being, wisdom, power, holiness, justice, goodness and truth.

"From the Bible we learn that in the beginning God created the heavens and the earth. He said, 'Let there be light,' and there was light: He laid the foundations of the earth; He bound up the waters in the thick clouds; He gave the sea a decree that it should not pass its bounds; He set a compass upon the great deep—He stretched out the North over the empty place, and hung the earth upon nothing. He made the beasts of the earth, and the fowls of the air, and every living creature that moveth upon the earth or in the waters. Last and best, He made man in His own image, and after His own likeness, and gave him dominion over every living thing. He gives the rain in due season, and the plentiful harvest. He shuts up the heavens and the earth yields not its fruit. From the Bible we learn that the Lord is God in Heaven above and in earth beneath. He will not justify the wicked, nor clear the guilty; but He is merciful and gracious, long suffering, and abundant in goodness and truth: Heaven is His throne and the earth is His footstool. The cattle upon a thousand hills are His,—the earth and the fulness thereof.

"I am a God at hand, saith the Lord, and not afar off. Can any hide himself in a secret place, that I shall not see him? Is there any darkness or shadow of death where the workers of iniquity may hide themselves? He is also very near to the righteous, as He declares His eyes are upon them, and His ears open to their complaints. The Bible was designed to save the world. Paul says the Gospel of Christ is the power of God unto salvation. All Scripture is given by inspiration, and is profitable for doctrine, for reproof, for correction and instruction; it contains all necessary rules for religious faith and practice. Paul said: 'If any man speak, let him speak as the oracles of God;' but in these latter days there has been a great departure from this. Men have tried to legislate for the church—have hewn out broken cisterns which hold no water. The people calling themselves *Christians* have seen the error of this—have renounced their men-made creeds and articles of faith, confessed their errors, and taken the Bible as their rule of faith and practice, with no name but *Christian*, and no test of fellowship but Christian character. I pray God that they, as a people, may never depart from this, or be guilty of teaching for doctrines the commandments of men; but may contend earnestly for the faith once delivered to the saints. Another object of the Bible is to encourage the saints. It abounds with such promises as these: 'Where two or three are gathered together in My name, there am I in the midst,' 'I will be with you always, even to the end of the world.' God has ever been with the faithful. He was with Noah in the ark; with Moses in the wilderness; with the Hebrew children in the fiery furnace, and with Daniel in the lions' den. He has caused these things to be recorded in His Book for our encouragement, and promised that He will be with His children in six troubles, and in the seventh that He will not desert them. 'Who shall be able to separate us from the love of Christ? Shall tribulation, or distress, or famine, or persecution? Nay: in all these things we shall be more than conquerors through Him that loved us! I am persuaded that neither life nor death, nor principalities, nor powers, nor things present, nor things to come, nor height, nor depth, nor any other creature, shall separate us from the love of God which is in Christ Jesus our Lord.'

"The Bible should be read by all. Were it not for this Holy Volume, we should be no better off than the idolators to whom Paul preached on Mars Hill. It points to God and says: 'This is life eternal, that they might know Thee, the only true God, and Jesus Christ whom Thou hast sent!'

"In the Bible we have not only the theory of religion, but we have religion itself, embodied and enlivened by living examples. There is not a single virtue which can adorn human life—not a grace that beautifies the heart, which has not been exemplified in some living character of the Bible. Thus we see faith in Abraham, meekness in Moses, wisdom in Solomon, patience in Job, zeal in Peter, and perseverance in Paul. In Jesus Christ we see all the graces that can adorn the life: all the perfections of Christianity How pleasant His delivery: what profound wisdom in His sermons; how spotless His life; what command over His passions; what patience under suffering; what triumph in death! Who could so live and so die? Surely never man spake like Him! He is the model for our imitation; let us keep Him continually before our eyes, and imitate Him as far as feeble human nature can. Search the Scriptures, for in them ye think ye have eternal life, and 'Whoso looketh into the perfect law of liberty, and continueth therein, being not a forgetful hearer, but a doer of the Word, that man shall be blessed in his deed.'

"In conclusion, I would recommend to all the Bible, I would recommend every one to become a student of the Bible, and form his life by its precepts. No other book can take its place. No other book can show the way to sins forgiven, or lead a step beyond the grave.

'" Let all the heathen writers join
  To make one perfect book—
Great! God when once compared with thine
  How mean their writings look.'"

"Thomas Henry."

THE SUPPORT OF THE GOSPEL.

"Support the ministry! Supply the necessary means for defraying Church expenses; or neither yourself, or church, or minister will prosper! Our great want is a spirit of devotedness and self-denial. 'Seek first the kingdom of heaven' is the Divine injunction, but we seem almost to have reversed the order; we seek every thing else first. Business must be enlarged, farms paid for and improved, money let out at interest, aye more, our dress and surroundings and equipage must all be elegant, before we can pay what is justly due to the church or minister. We need not attempt to excuse ourselves by saying, 'We pay all we *sign*.' Refusing to *sign* does not absolve us from the obligation to support the gospel. When we make a profession of religion, we thereby assume the obligation to support that religion. When we become members of a church, we bind ourselves in so doing, to the support of that church. Let us see to it that we discharge our duty in this particular. We mourn over the desolation of Zion, but where is the cause? Does not the sin lie at our own door? Can we expect to see new churches spring up, or weak churches grow into strong ones, while wealthy brethren hoard up their gold or let it out at usury, instead of liberally paying their ministers? There are men who pay by *fives* and *tens* who might give by *hundreds* without abridging the comforts or even luxuries of their families in the least. The only difference they would feel at the end of the year, would be in the amount of interest to be put out at interest again. There are others who might pay liberally if they were not slaves to passion. But a certain *style* must be maintained whether God's cause is maintained or not, Let us see if we are not guilty on this point. In this unjustifiable strife for outward adornment, do we not consume the offerings which should be laid on the altar of our God? If we exhaust the utmost farthing of our income on expensive dress and furniture, where shall we find means to support the Gospel?

" There are young men among us, not only willing but anxious to enter the ministry—young men who would be useful, and who in the hands of other denominations would soon be used, who remain inactive, because no opening presents itself. They cannot meet the wants of our churches, or of the community at large without further preparation. That preparation they cannot make, and at the same time maintain themselves and families. Some one will say, 'Go forth without farther preparation as did our pioneers. They were unlettered men, yet they built up our churches.' If any one takes this advice, and comes to talk to us a little on Sunday, after a week spent in manual labor, the chances are, that our fastidious brethren will turn from him with ill-concealed disgust. He will go home discouraged, and begin to doubt its being his duty to try to preach at all. At the same time other denominations are inviting them to attractive fields of labor, and offering them salaries which would enable them to discharge their duties, with credit to themselves and the church with which they labored. Are we less wealthy than these other denominations, or do we love the cause less? God forbid that the latter should be the case; yet a visit to the sumptuous homes which abound in most of our churches, would seem to disprove the former.

" But if we are less liberal with our ministers than some other denominations around us, we are not less exacting. I know a wealthy church of a denomination that I could mention, that listens once a month to a local preacher, far inferior to those whom we snub occasionally, that its regular preachers may extend their labors. Yet this church pays a salary which none of our churches in Canada pay. Men among us who pay ten or twenty dollars a year, will talk about talented ministers, as though they thought a Beecher, or Spurgeon should be obtained for three or four hundred dollars a year. If we want talented men we must pay the sums that will command talent. 'But,' says one, 'if men are called of God to preach, they will go where they can do most good, not where they are best paid.' Very true! But a man has every reason to believe he can best serve God and do good where he is best appreciated. If we were too poor to pay our ministers, I would say, woe to him who being called, forsakes us for the loaves and fishes.

" When this Province was new and our people poor and few, the word grew and was multiplied, though little was given. That little was like the widow's mite—all they had, and God blessed it accordingly.

Let us give as much in proportion to what we have now, as they give then, and see if our Father will not pour us out an overflowing cup of blessing.

"Let us pay the ministers we have such salaries as will enable them to cultivate their powers properly, and it is quite probable we shall find that they possess a higher order of talent than we have supposed they did.

"What I have said, I have said in a spirit of kindness. Let us examine ourselves and see if we are doing what we can. Are we laying up treasures in Heaven, or do our treasures accumulate only on earth? Wealthy brethren, ye who deal in large per-centages, I will tell you of a good investment. Lend to the Lord. He pays compound interest and the principal is sure."

A SHORT SERMON.

"And the Lord aid unto Noah, Come thou and all thy house into the ark."—Gen. vii. 1.

"The ark was the only place of safety—a colossal floating house, made of gopher wood (probably cypress), containing small rooms or cells, and pitched within and without.

"Noah and others, undoubtedly, had preached a long time, year after year, to the antediluvians; but they were incorrigible. Their cup of wickedness was full. 'God saw that the wickedness of man was great in the earth, and that every imagination of the thoughts of his heart was only evil continually. And it repented the Lord that He had made man on the earth.'

"And the Lord had previously declared, 'My Spirit shall not always strive with man.'

"What an awful state of things, only one pious family in all the world, the whole earth filled with violence—the measure of their iniquities filled up! God had been merciful and longsuffering, but is about to show Himself a God of judgment now. 'But Noah found grace in the eyes of the Lord, and was called by Himself to come into the ark, him and his house.' They were shut in, and the wicked shut out.

" Noah prepared the ark with his own hands, according to the Divine direction, of course. All is ready for the terrible voyage. A solemn pause. 'For yet seven days, and I will cause it to rain upon the earth forty days and forty nights.' A week for a world to repent! Alas, what perverseness, what reckless disregard! they only laugh until the awful dispensation bursts upon them.

"Now, Jesus Christ is the only ark of safety whereby WE can be saved. The door is open, and Jesus Christ, by the grace of God, tasted death for every man. (Heb. ii. 9.)

" He invites and calls all: 'Come unto me, all ye that labor and are heavy laden, and I will give you rest. Take my yoke upon you, and learn of me; for I am meek and lowly in heart: and ye shall find rest unto your souls.' The apostles were commissioned to 'go into all the world, and preach the gospel to every creature. He that believeth, and is baptized, shall be saved.' The Church, which is figuratively called the Bride, says, 'Come.' The Spirit says, 'Come. And let him that heareth say, Come. And let him that is athirst Come. And whosoever will, let him take of the water of life freely.'

"Thousands have come, and found grace, and others are coming. The door of mercy is still open, and the blood of Christ still cleanses from all sin.

" But there are those amongst us that make light of the invitation and command, and say, there is time enough yet. It was so with the antediluvians until the door was shut, and the flood came; then their cries were in vain. Will it not be so with those who refuse offered grace, and disobey the gospel? Thus it was with the people of Sodom and Gomorrah. The Jewish nation also rejected the Son of God, and cried, 'Away with Him; and, crucify Him!' When Jerusalem was surrounded by the Roman army, and the judgments of God about to fall upon them, there was a respite, and the wise fled; then the door was shut.

"Good news is now preached to Jew and Gentile. The faithful minister teaches,admonishes and prays,the tears flow and the exhortations are heard; we have line upon line, precept upon precept, here a little and there a little; yet many say, by their acts if not in words, there is time enough yet; when I have a more convenient season, I will call for thee.

"Dear reader, listen to my last remark, believe it is said in love. Listen to the remark of one who has seen much of life. I fear that many are refusing offered mercy, and will refuse until the door is shut, and will take up the sad lament at last: 'The harvest is past, the summer is ended and we are not saved.'

"'Come to the ark, come to the ark,
To Jesus come away;
The pestilence walks forth by night,
The arrow flies by day.'"

"Port Oshawa, Dec. 2, 1866."

The following peculiar and interesting letter I found among Father Henry's papers:

"East Avon, N. Y., 2nd of 9th month, 1853.
"Eld. Thomas Henry,—

"Agreeable to your request, I hereby send you, as far as may be, an answer to the questions: 'How came the Christians to come to Canada? Wh came? and when? When and where was the first church formed? To answer the first question, I will make extracts from a letter of Eld. D. Millard, dated July 10th, 1821.' 'I have received a letter from a sister now residing in the village of Newmarket, Township of Whitchurch, about thirty miles North of Little York, Upper Canada. She was an early fruit of my labor in the gospel, and I baptized her in Greenville, N. Y., in the summer of 1817. She shortly after moved with her husband to the place where she now lives. Having heard of free brethren in Niagara Co., N. Y., she has written the most urgent requests, for some free preachers to come to that place.

"This letter, which gave me the first information of her exact place of residence, was directed to Bros. Brown of Porter, N. Y., and handed to me a few days since. My young travelling brethren, let my entreaties go with our sisters for some one to embark!

"Mary Stogdill to T. Brown. Dear Brother, Having an opportunity, I again take my pen, fearing my second letter never reached you, as I have heard nothing from you since your first letter; and that is a long time. Eld. Doubleday has never seen me. Bro. McIntyre has never visited us, although most anxiously have I looked for them. Think how great the disappointment, yet I still hope. Oh, persuade them to come! Tell them Paul sought other countries, that he might not build on another's foundation. Bid them God speed to this part of the vineyard, for the fields are white and ready to harvest. Have you seen Eld. Millard this winter? Perhaps he would come if he knew where to find us. I long for brethren, being such a tender lamb when I was transplanted from the flock at Greenville. Come in, ye heralds of the Cross, and Jesus come with you."

See *C. Herald*, vol. 4, No. 2, Aug. 16th, 1821. "Before the close of the month, Bro. A. Huntly presented himself at her door. It so happened that Darius Man, of Lake Simcoe, was at her house at the time, and invited him to go to the Lake, where God soon blessed his labors, as may be seen by an extract from Eld. Baily's letter of Oct. 31st, 1821." Pomfret N. Y., " Bro. Allen Huntly gave us (the Conference) an account of his travels and success in preaching the gospel in Upper Canada, where he had been laboring; being led to visit that place by a letter from Sister Stogdill, published in the *Herald.*

"He also presented us a letter from a number of brethren in North Gwillimsbury near Lake Simcoe, U. C. The Conference took the matter into consideration, and it seemed, after much prayer, good to us to send chosen men with Bro. Huntly, that they might set in order the things that were wanting. And the Spirit bade Eld. Simeon Bishop and myself go with him, nothing doubting. We embarked at Fort George, and after a tempestuous voyage landed at Little York. We went from thence to Simcoe, where we saw the grace of God and were glad.

"On the first day of the week, being the 21st of Oct., almost the whole of the settlement came together, and we ordained Bro. Huntly, after which he repaired to the Lake, where there was much water, and he baptized ten happy converts; then we returned to the house, and organized a church of forty-three names in New Testament order.

"Thus you will see, that the first Ordination, the first Baptism, and the first Church organization in U. C., took place on the 21st of Oct., 1821.

"The next June, Bro. Huntly came to a General Meeting in West Bloomfield, N. Y., and said : 'I have now left Canada, and cannot return there to stay, but I ask that the church there have immediate help. If it does it may be saved, if not it will go down.' The chief speaker then arose and said: 'Who will volunteer for Canada?' All were silent.

O I wished in my heart that I was fit to go. With streaming eyes he repeated the question. Again there was no response. 'Shall we,' said he, 'like hirelings, sacrifice this lonely flock to ravenous wolves? Is there not a David among us?' I could remain seated no longer, but arose and said I would go, if I could have one to go with me. A. C. Morrison arose and said he would be the one to go with me.

"We were neither of us ordained, but after some talk and much prayer, Bro. Morrison was ordained. We arrived at Lake Simcoe on the 15th of 7th month, 1822. Though the waves rose high, and terrible was the tempest, yet he who said, 'Peace! be still!' spoke calmness to the heart. Gently died the tempest—and smoothed were the waves; and there was a great calm. On the 20th of 11th month, 1822, a church was formed in East Gwillimsbury, which was the second church formed in the Province. I have now tried to redeem my promise, but if I have fallen short, ask and I will try again.

"Yours as ever,

"NATHAN HARDING."

The following poems by the author are appended to this work by request. The first refers to my own father, Elder Joshua Hayward, who died in 1840, after twenty-three years of laborious work in the Gospel field. The second to my mother, Mrs. Lydia Hayward, who still lives, though now in her ninety-second year, and enjoys good health and the use of all her faculties.

IN MEMORIAM.

How long it is since father died!
How many years,
Since I a child stood by his side
And brushed his hair?

And travelling through those misty years,
　　Has made me old;
My brow is seamed, and silver hairs
　　Replace the gold.

Has father since that far off time
　　A stranger grown;
Or would he in that "happy clime"
　　His daughter own?

My father, by thy side to-night
　　I seem to stand,
To brush again thy locks of white
　　With tender hand.

How little then my childish heart
　　Could know of thine;
Our forms so near, so far apart
　　Thy soul from mine.

Though Death's dark stream between us roll,
　　We're nearer now;
Father, I stand beside thy soul,
　　And touch thy brow.

Thy solemn consecrated life
　　I understand;
In scenes of weariness and strife
　　I take thy hand.

I see thee in thy country's need
　　Where armies meet;
I see thee lay that country's meed
　　At Jesus' feet.

Devoting all thy manhood's powers
　　To do His will,
Through weary years and toilsome hours
　　His soldier still.

Tis' well! thy work was nobly done
　　God gave thee rest,
Ere yet thy life's declining sun
　　Had touched the west.

TO MY MOTHER ON HER NINETIETH BIRTHDAY.

As floats the vessel down the river
  Towards the deep wide-rolling sea,
So glides our life-barque onward ever
  Towards the great eternity.

At first we sail o'er silver sands,
  On a small stream through shady bowers,
Still reaching out with eager hands
  To grasp the wayside fruits and flowers.

And still we glide adown the stream,
  That deepens, widens, resteth never
Till in the noon-day sun's hot gleam,
  We're floating on a mighty river.

Mid rocks and reefs and waterfalls,
  Borne on by the resistless tide;
Fearful and faint our spirit calls,
  What hand shall help, what pilot guide?

The rocks are past, the sun sinks low,
  We hold the helm with weary hands;
The deepening stream with measured flow
  Makes mournful music on the sands.

Cool shadows gather in the West,
  The vessel worn with seam and scar,
Is drifting on the river's breast,
  But whole in every sail and spar.

Solemn prophetic whispers say,
  Oh, waiting soul, the end is near;
The voyage shall end and close the day,
  But not, dear heart, in doubt and fear.

The tired palms and aching brow
  Shall rest, for soon a stronger hand
Shall grasp the helm, and guide the prow
  The keel shall touch the silver sand.

The loved and loving ones now gone
  Who made the voyage of life before,
In day that needs not sun or moon,
  Shall come to greet thee on the shore.

RETROSPECTION.

The past, the long and weary past,
Has lengthened shadows o'er it cast,
By life's now slowly, setting sun,
Of all I've said and thought and done.

And looking back along the road,
Which my unwary feet have trod,
I see how oft I've turned aside,
Blinded by passion, or by pride;

Or, hurrying eagerly along,
Have left the *little* good undone;
Or crushed beneath my stumbling feet,
Jewels rare and blossoms sweet;

Neglecting, in my foolish haste,
The cooling, way-side spring to taste,
Whose waters, sweetly bubbling up,
Might fill contentment's homely cup.

I strove in doubt, sometimes in tears,
To fill with good those buried years;
With anxious thought and eager sight,
Wearily searching for the right.

I looked away, too high, too far,
Dazzled by some uncertain star;
With busy head and hands I wrought,
Yet seldom found the thing I sought.

I mourn the seed I left unsown;
The kindly deeds I might have done;
The loving words I failed to say;
Each wasted hour, and misspent day.

And yet those years were not all lost,
Not wholly barren in the past:
Some precious seed was ripened there;
Some days were peaceful, bright, and fair.

The sun has always shone above,
And over all brooded God's love;
And in His hands my past I leave,
And to His care my future give.

NEARER THEE.

Nearer to Thee, O God I'd come
A tired child away from home;—
Weary with wandering far and wide,
With ills beset on every side.
O Father, hear thy pleading child!
The wilderness is waste and wild;
Fierce storms are howling o'er the lea.
Oh take me Father nearer thee!

The visions of life's early day
Have faded from my sight away;
The song that charmed my youthful years,
Has died upon my listless ears;
This changing and uncertain life
Is full of vanity and strife:
And from the conflict wearily,
Thy worried child comes nearer Thee!

I heard Thy voice above the storm,
Calling the foolish wanderer home;
Like Noah's dove, I'd sought for rest,
But sought in vain. Now to Thy breast
Gladly I come. Lo! here is peace!
Thy voice can bid the tumult cease,
Thy arm of love encircles me,
Yet still my prayer is, "Nearer Thee."

I heard Thy voice above the storm,
Calling the foolish wanderer home.
Like Noah's dove, I'd sought for rest,
But sought in vain. Now to Thy breast
Gladly I come. Lo! here is peace!
Thy voice can bid the tumult cease,
Thy arm of love enriches me,
Yet still my prayer is, "Nearer Thee."

HILL & WEIR, PRINTERS, TEMPERANCE ST., TORONTO.

www.ingramcontent.com/pod-product-compliance
Lightning Source LLC
Chambersburg PA
CBHW020844160426
43192CB00007B/777